*The Beginning of Wisdom
Is Wonder!*

Proverbs 9:10

THE SPIRITUAL
DANCE OF LIFE

Where Two Worlds Meet

THE SPIRITUAL DANCE OF LIFE

Where Two Worlds Meet

By

M. Teri Daunter, Ph.D.

MOBIUS PUBLISHING
Petoskey, Michigan

For information address: Mobius Publishing
Post Office Box 2457
Petoskey, MI 49770

Library of Congress Catalog-in-Publication Data

M. Teri Daunter, Ph.D.
The Spiritual Dance of Life
Where Two Worlds Meet
   First edition
Mobius Publishing January 1995

1. Psychology   2. Science
3. Evolution/Philosophy 4. Past Life Therapy

I. Title

ISBN 0-9643646-8-9 HD   CIP
ISBN 0-9643646-9-7 PBK   94-96592

DEDICATION

To Jim, Kelly, and Dominic
*There have been no greater gifts in my life
than the three of you.*

To Dana, Chad and Chene Allen
*You have made the rainbows in my life
shine so much brighter*

To my Mother and Father
*I thank you for the gift of life
Special love and admiration
goes to both of you.*

CONTENTS

CONTENTS

ACKNOWLEDGMENTS

Many people contributed through their encourage-ment to the writing and completion of *The Spiritual Dance of Life*, which was created at a very deep metaphysical level, so that I am as intrigued by it as anyone else. I owe my eternal gratitude to one special individual, Dr. Charles L. Spiegel, an unwavering friend, master of initiative and inspiration, and a brilliant scholar who has had a ripple effect internationally. He has been a support and a kin-dred spirit to me through his editing wizardry of every page of the book. Furthermore, I applaud him for books he has authored on the continuity of consciousness, which are transforming the lives of people everywhere throughout the world. I respect him for the example he sets!

I also thank Margaret Charette and Carol Robinson, the typographers, whose unstinting commitment to the retyping of the many edits of this book made all of this possible. I thank them from the bottom of my heart. I thank Laura Taylor Cherven for her creativity and assistance with the cover design.

I especially thank my family, Jim, Kelly, Dominic, Dana and Chad Daunter for their patience and unstinting commitment throughout the many weeks of writing of this book, and to whom this book is dedicated. You are all locked deeply in my heart.

I am indebted to Robert Leonhardt, O.F.M. and John Rohe, J.D. for their grammatical expertise and review. Their punctuation of the manuscript was an important help in the completion of this work.

Finally, and above all, I thank the great Spirits who inspired and guided this book, an instance of multidimensional art. They walked with me every step of the way and acted as my polarity. This book is from them, and about them, the ascended Masters, my overshadowing forces. It is my awareness of the overshadowing presence of these spiritual Beings that will be the guiding influence in my life's work!

FOREWORD

The grand design of life as a continuity of consciousness from life to life, and the development of one's higher potential, is the statement of this remarkable book on spiritual transformation!

Dr. M. Teri Daunter's pioneering, landmark book, *The Spiritual Dance of Life - Where Two Worlds Meet*, speaks of the reality of consciousness as an expression of the spiritual design of life! It is in the understanding of the ebb and flow of consciousness, that the dilemmas and enigmas of life will be answered by the truth seeker!

The spiritual reality of each individual, as a reflection of an infinite creative intelligence, is the necessary fulcrum by which we can open the door and let light illuminate the problem in which we are encased from our life-to-life experiences. Dr. Daunter describes the science of healing as a *science of life*, in which it is the responsibility of each person to recognize how one's own distress was caused through a lack of understanding of the dynamics of the continuity of consciousness from life to life.

With case studies from her clinical practice, Dr. Daunter provides illuminating information, revealing that the cause of any mental and physical malfunction is derived from previous lives lived by the individual. The central statement of this book is that all disease is a reflection of one's mental attitude which, as a result, creates the distress that is experienced in one's present life. Dr. Daunter helps us to understand the shifts we must make in attitude and consciousness.

We are all concerned with healing! Distraught individuals first look to the healer, the physician, psychiatrist, psychologist, and other therapies. He does not recognize that he can heal himself! However, one can heal oneself when one is able to diagnose the disease. To be able to diagnose one's disease and to heal oneself, mandates an understanding of the physics and the psychology of consciousness. Of great importance is the awareness of one's thoughts, because such thoughts contain the negative or positive ingredients of one's past life experiences which are constantly molding one's present environment.

In our everyday walk of life, we cannot associate ourselves with any immediate view of life about us without involving ourselves in the same frequency relationship, which originally created that particular situation, any more than we can attune a radio or television to a broadcasting station without the direct result of receiving the program being broadcast.

All people are transceivers, that is to say that they are transmitting and receiving signals from the past, the present and the future. The future is, to all intents and purposes, the fourth and higher dimension.

FOREWORD

Dr. Daunter explains the *electronic tuning process* as an interdimensional principle of frequency relationship. The obsessive factors that have entered a person's life from past lifetimes are established again in the present life. Thus, every individual's present life is folded within hundreds, if not thousands, of previous life experiences from the past.

In this book, *The Spiritual Dance of Life*, Dr. Daunter, a profound thinker with a depth of wisdom and an expansive vision, illustrates how all persons, in reality, live on two worlds - the third-dimensional material worlds, constructed from experiences lived from past lifetimes and being relived in the present, as well as fourth-dimensional spiritual worlds in which positive information was gained about the life cycle.

This is a revolutionary book about the spiritual nature of life and of progressive evolution which transcends the customary boundaries. The reader will take a giant step forward when learning how to apply this healing science to remove those obstacles that have hindered spiritual expression!

The reality of Love, Dr. Daunter states, is the ultimate expression of an Infinite Creative Intelligence. Love is everything and there is nothing else but Love! Dr. Daunter handles big issues in a compassionate, sincere, direct, and loving way. This author is truly her own person and does her own thinking uncontaminated by societal and cultural illusions. *The Spiritual Dance of Life* is a tremendous piece of literary work whose voice will ripple its effects for decades to come.

Dr. Charles L. Spiegel, Director
Unarius Academy of Science
El Cajon, California

Our lives begin to end
About the day we become silent
About the things that matter.

Author Unknown

PROLOGUE

We are children when it comes to understanding the true nature of the mind. Mind is an infinity of vibration. *The Spiritual Dance of Life* moves us from the roots of orthodox thinking and presents a theory of consciousness out of new understanding of the interdimensional concepts of the life cycle. A psychology of consciousness is described which encourages us to clear our past in order to accelerate our spiritual evolution. The information contained herein pushes us to wake up to who we really are in order to shift past traumas into transcendencies where new energies begin to flow through us. The earth world is a work-out world which enables us to remove the obstacles which interfere with our spiritual development.

The Spiritual Dance of Life stresses the enormous powers our beliefs have and how our education and culture cause our extraordinary abilities to atrophy. It presents a hopeful and endearing new dimension to such controversial topics as life, death, birth, and the after-life. It communicates clearly that the purpose of life is to evolve and learn and that multiple rebirths facilitate that process. Profound psychological and physical healings occur from unearthing traumatic past-life experiences. *The Spiritual Dance of Life* asserts the deeper meanings behind coincidences and "accidental" events. We create our life experiences at a very deep metaphysical subconscious level in order that we meet people from whom we need to learn. They occur to lead us forward in our spiritual development.

The outer trappings of our life are insignificant. They are compensatory activities which leave us feeling apathetic. It is inner growth that matters. Therefore, we need to cherish what calls out to us whether or not it is valued by the culture because orthodox culture is a pale shadow of a deeper order.

The Spiritual Dance of Life is a guide for cultivating depth, breadth, and spirituality in everyday life. It encourages us to live at a level of higher consciousness and to honor our own inner experience. It is a reliable map for the journey of the soul.

*I*NTRODUCTION

"If you cannot - in the long run - tell everyone what you have been doing, your doing has been worthless" commented Erwin Schrodinger, a Viennese physicist. This book has been written in the spirit of sharing my earnest search for truth. This book is a synthesis of my spiritual Odyssey, it is the wisdom of age, an inward quest, a continuous process of enlightenment. My intention is to distill helpful insights about spiritual evolution through the scientific understanding of man's infinite nature to change and reveal his interior and spiritually creative design. It is an attempt to present in a precise logical manner the extraordinary process which is occurring in spiritual life-rhythms.

I have pondered through many stages in my thoughts about life, about God, and about spirituality. There are many pathways by which we can achieve a high state of spiritual evolution and inner serenity. Yet all of these pathways, can be facilitated by the understanding of the interdimensional physics of energy; different strategies, yet one goal.

We need to continuously seek and explore healthy successful resolutions toward this goal, as there are extreme polarities of positive and negative energy present in current world conditions. No one can dispute that there are many manifest diseases afflicting our body and soul. It is this whirling of energy and objective in breaking through the discord, that my exploration has led to my present discovery. In no way, however, is my search concluded.

Through the understanding of the physics of energy, I have discovered a pathway to Infinite Creative Intelligence that is intellectually satisfying to my wrestling spirit. As I have grown in maturity, insight, and experience, I have learned that the Consciousness of each one of us is the Consciousness of the Infinite. Infinite Creative Intelligence is the total *energy dance* of the universe with both its positive and negative aspects. Creation is regenerative in form and substance. Every part and process of our being and experience is a microcosm of the Infinite. This substance runs through everything and is eternal. Life is a hologram. God is not a singular entity but energy composed of countless tissues of light. Man is a singular reflection of energy!

I no longer can conceive of a world that is only in design finite; a world in which the Infinite Creative Intelligence interferes capriciously with our destiny and spiritual evolution. Rather we evolve through an interdimensional regenerative life cycle. I can no longer conceive of a God who will completely annihilate His own creation by shutting the door completely at the end of one cycle after such long continued progress and when we are just of age and becoming fit to live. Our talents and experiences develop slowly, and if we are to grow in the Infinite's image and likeness we need to experience infinite opportunities, not one brief cycle of incarnation. How absurd to create man in such magnificence only to silence him eternally after a split second of the cosmic clock!

We do not die! Our spirit lives throughout many lives. Simply to assert that this is not true because it cannot be proven by third-dimensional science is an unintuitive response. As psychologists, we depend on countless phenomena for diagnostic conclusions that we cannot scientifically explain but interpret each time we administer assessment instruments. We believe we comprehend ideas by looking at numbers, blots, and marks on a page. These interpretive phenomena are accepted by the judicial system as opinions premised upon scientific knowledge that satisfy standards of evidentiary reliability. Such opinions cannot be subjected to scientific scrutiny; yet they are designated and accepted as indisputable fact.

Scientists frequently admit their inability to explain completely such phenomena as DNA, the brain and memory, as they cannot yet fathom their inner workings. Our naked eyes are incapable of visualizing infra-red and ultra-violet rays. Yet we know that these spectrums exist. Our ears are incapable of perceiving the frequency of sound available to most animals. Our ears are attuned to only a few of the sound waves that are constantly beating upon our eardrums. Very short waves and very long ones are entirely imperceptible to us. Certain birds perceive the magnetic grid of the earth and use it for migration. The same with light. Light waves of very high or very low frequency cannot be detected by our unaided eyes despite the fact that they are there all the time. So an interdimensional universe involving past lives is possible and probable beyond the perception of human capabilities.

We can no longer dismiss the interdimensional concepts of the life cycle without revealing plain lack of scholarship and deep inquiry. The sensation of a unified transactional field fits the facts of experiential life. To think otherwise is a deprivation of logic and reason and a dangerous hallucination. Our world is a world of individual perceptions built on memory, fear, anxiety, and desire. A multilife perspective is not a religious belief system but a scientific fact of predictable patterns. It is a spiritual technology of self-cultivation.

Similar concepts existed in Christianity until the sixth century when they were banned by a special council in Constantinople under the Emperor Justinian in connection with the teachings of Father Origen. Rebirth philosophy was nearly universal in ancient and pre-industrial cultures and is the cornerstone of the great Indian spiritual systems and a broad spectrum of other cultures.

Life is full of mysteries. We need to be open-minded if we are going to understand the smallest fraction of this mystery. Without receptivity, we cannot hear the teacher of our inner voice. Progressive growth through receptivity will not happen all at once, but through deliberate effort and learning. In these efforts we will make errors. Errors are essential to improvement. Something is only a mistake if we don't learn from it; if we learn from it, it becomes a positive experience. Every experience challenges us to call on the best that is within us. The course and tenor of our spiritual life is determined by how well we listen to our inner voice. Yet this inner voice has its polarity, the inner enemy, the dark side or lower self, which is in constant dialectical process with our higher consciousness. This juxtaposition is designed to aid us in discovering our own empowerment in the midst of our karmic workshop.

We live in a world that ignores spirit by influencing our minds with plastic thoughts and discursive chatter. Such incessant dialogues and propaganda entrench us in prisons of self-created limitations and sterile fixations as we gaze outward for direction. These heaps of conventions and habits of which society has made us, drown out the inner voice of growth by creating fixed mental patterns and a collective hypnosis which we call reality. The answers are within ourselves. "The kingdom of God is within", Jesus continuously instructed us. We must tap our inner selves in order to see the light. We must open our eyes and stop living our lives through someone else's dream. Anyone who demands that there is only one path Home is teaching you fear. This type of indiscriminate 'help' is violence against spirit. To think intelligently for ourselves is the beginning of true spirituality. We haven't worn the same size shoes we wore when we were two years old. Yet we continue to squeeze ourselves uncomfortably into concepts which no longer fit. Where do you think so many of your tensions come from? From trying to force yourself into something which no longer fits and which has become for you obsolete. The goal of existence is to "be" without conditioning because this mental norm is dramatically constricted. Once you allow for new thinking, you will be relieved of an incredible burden. Our spirit cannot be built on surrender nor on submission. It needs to be based on confidence and inner knowledge. It is a force requiring our collaboration in the future evolution of a spirit-centered world!

It is important, however, that we do not become over-fascinated with past life recall and view it as some extraordinary event. Past life recall in itself does not necessarily make one spiritual. So in evaluating spiritual paths the criterion is not psychic phenomenon but a path motivated by a lifewalk of selflessness, generosity, sensitivity and tolerance in the service of man. The spiritual path is a transcending of the ego. Every decision we make either supports or disturbs our spirituality. Intellectual decisions motivate us towards positive purposes.

Debate about whether or not the experience of past lives exist is pointless. That is tantamount to asking whether my sensation and experience of love is the same as yours. But the experience is not pointless because when one has even one past life experience, one's way of living is transformed. Such an experiential referent makes sense of life and individuals change in a profound way by improving their ethical actions and emotional habits. The purpose of living life finally becomes perfectly clear. Past-life work, therefore, is not about symptom reduction, it is about our spirituality, about infinite possibilities and un-manifested potential. The therapeutic results I have observed in my clinical practice through past life therapy transcended any other methodology. It surpasses months of conventional treatment because health is all about spirituality, the absence of disease! As a psychologist, one shifts from seeing people as clinical cases to souls on a journey. Past life memories touch people deeply and facilitate long-term change.

Past life study, then, is about the Christ Spirit of ordinary human beings. It is the perennial and numinous philosophy of our existence that we emerge with some variation again and again in different settings. It is the

Self searching for itself. It is about recognizing that every human effort has the potential to draw us back to the Infinite so that "I and the Father are one," as Jesus clearly related. Jesus had an enormous spiritual vision. He made it clear that we are a part of the whole. Just as the brain is responsible for the energy expressed in every cell of our being, and that every component part is an expression of the whole, so are we an expression of Infinity, the electromagnetic flux field of the universe. We are of the same basic spiritual identity. This Infinite sense of true Oneness is our Consciousness and our inspiration to progress.

To become a spiritual being, requires that we cleanse our doors of false perceptions in order to see the message of the Creative Infinite in every moment of our life. Every thought, event, or feeling carries the touch of the Infinite. In our fear and desperation we run and hide behind answers in conventional patterns. We fear suffering at the whim of some greater power. Our spirituality will come into play in the act of dancing in the infinite present. This dance is not mastered in an orderly linear process. Sometimes it eludes us. Other times we circle around with uncertainty. However, it is like a hologram. First we cannot see it; then we *cannot not* see it. It requires deliberate effort and attention to our thought processes and intuition.

The dance of spirituality is most gracefully accomplished through the vision opened to us by a fuller understanding of the interdimensional concepts of the life cycle. We need to dance often and well. The highest music of this divine dance is past life study. The preludes and fugues of past life work are simply a complex arrangement of divine Wisdom. The intricate melodies flow on and on. Inferior music depletes spiritual energy since it originates from human purpose. Eternity is manifest in this symphony of life which Saint Francis of Assisi, an early proponent of nonlocal mind, tried to bring into our consciousness. Whenever this dance begins to overshadow our thoughts, we expel it out of fear of the unknown and continue to merely bow and kneel to protocol, as if in a Court.

Past life therapy is a god-like extravaganza, positively biased, tapping into the vastness of our infinite capabilities. It is a gateway to a special kind of self knowledge. It is an inner-world adventure into the inner frontiers of consciousness. It is a homeopathic move to go mentally with what is always an inherent and available attribute of mankind. It is mind expanding and encouraging us to look at principles operating beyond the common view.

Whether you look at past life work as your own personal history, ancestral memories, or part of the collective consciousness, nevertheless, it is your own mind which draws these images and experiences to the surface for a purpose. Therefore, the distilled essence of the experience, rather than the exactness of a recall, is therapeutically valid. Significant healing can be realized when knowledge gained is skillfully utilized. However the outlook, the recall aids in unblocking significant energy within an individual. This is why my position about past lives in therapy is objective. This objectivity allows each individual to view his experience in whatever philosophical orientation is useful for him. Personally, I have experienced numerous relivings. Therefore, I believe I have lived other lifetimes previous to my present life.

Past life study provides one with the psychic fuel to become a spiritual athlete and explore the minefield of his mind in a boundless process of existence. It is a sacred act that assists you in becoming the curator of your spirit. Past life study when properly applied, is grounded spirituality. Anything less is dangerous and leads to obsessions. Individuals who are able to achieve past life recall, experience rapid spiritual development because past life work is a method by which we stop being someone we thought we were and become our True Self.

In these chapters I offer you my knowledge and my experiences in whatever way they may be useful to you. I merely wish to outline a natural approach to healing so as to attain spiritual maturity. The natural principles of the interdimensional life cycle will fill you with spiritual vitality, and aid you in exercising your spiritual muscles so they do not atrophy. The fact that you are reading this book is helping you stretch gently in preparation for the dance. Every page you read will expand your range of motion. It takes time to get in shape. So don't push the river.

My knowledge is not final. Truth is an infinite perspectus and much broader than any one individual can ever conceive. No one has a monopoly on truth except those insisting they are infallible and believe they are invariably right. Such unenlightened people risk premature hardening of their mental and spiritual arteries.

The Spiritual Dance of Life provides uncommonly useful tools to help one reframe reality, see the shadows on the wall, and maintain the inner balance of one's positive and negative voices. May this book be a beacon of light and lead the way for the widening of your consciousness by developing an undistorted life-affirming knowledge of your Infinite capabilities in your progressive evolution.

PART ONE

What lies behind us
and what lies before us
are tiny matters
compared to what lies within us.

Oliver Wendell Holmes

Chapter One

Principles Of Past Life Recall

Our daily life is a recombination of the past. We carry the imprint of our past with us at every moment. Everyone is living from the past. Not only do we carry the pattern, but the emotional experience as well becomes imprinted so that we carry it with us into our future lives. The harvests of one cycle, or one lifetime, are inherited as seeds of potentiality in the next lifetime. In other words, we inherit characteristics which we acquire as a result of our past action in previous lives. We progress through the course of many lifetimes accumulating past life experiences which are retained in our psychic anatomy, our consciousness.

This is reincarnation heredity. This heredity sets a framework of limitations into our present experiences in the third dimension. We inherit limitations or liberations which we generate in previous lifetimes. These inherited characteristics are transmitted from one lifetime into another reflecting the principle of cause and effect. Therefore, we create our own destiny. Our self-identity, then, extends through time and Infinity. This inherited pattern is the governing factor in past life recall.

Thus, past life experiences leave their mark upon our consciousness and create long standing personality patterns which can become problematic in one's daily life. These bleed-through experiences from past lives demonstrate themselves in our attractions, our likes and dislikes, and our resistances. We are constantly meeting ourselves. When we link an effect to its cause, we find that they manifest in cycles and extend through time into many lifetimes. Everything evolves out of a dynamic cycle. The cyclic interplay of these interdimensional forces of energy is the substance of past life studies. These studies require a basic knowledge of man's invisible nature and man's latent abilities!

All the forces of energy which evolve from our inter-dimensional abilities and the inheritances of the many incarnated lives, merge into the creation of choices we make in terms of parentage, place of birth, time of birth, and race. These forces unfold into the continuing experiences of our individual life. Nothing happens by accident. Everything evolves out of a direction which we set for ourselves.

The study of past life recall opens our path inward and extends us beyond the walls of birth and death. These walls imprison us in a single incarnation. We have a natural reluctance to be confined.

When you begin your study of past lives and begin to reach into your past life experiences, you will never be the same. You will become more aware that the threads of all forces, events, and consciousness are woven into an unparalleled net of infinite relations. The distinction between the outer world and the inner world breaks down completely. They are fused into a unified undifferentiated whole. Your two worlds will meet. Your individuality dissolves into the Infinite, an undifferentiated Oneness. We become One with the Infinite, as there is no meaning to life as an isolated entity. We can only understand ourselves when we see ourselves as interconnections with the Infinite. No matter what happens to you externally, you remain anchored internally through past life studies. The study of past life recall will begin to open up your pathway, to discover your soul. If a path does not reveal your soul, it is of no use.

Past life study is not for amusement. It is for individuals with a sincerity of heart in wanting to achieve a higher state in their evolutionary process, by learning to cancel out past life negations. Overcoming past life negations is a never-ending process because a lifetime does not stand in isolation. Each lifetime is the child of all your former lifetimes. Your present lifetime is the parent of the lives which will follow.

In studying past lives, the power of an all-illuminating insight must go hand in hand with a deep sense of humility and meekness of heart since what one finds out about past lives is not always sweet. With ordinary abilities and dauntless patience, inward reflection, and undisturbed conviction, however, you can become competent in past life studies. There is no fixed period of graduation as in public education.

Past life work is the work of living ideas; ideas that release the abilities and powers of the Spiritual Self rather than combining your consciousness into material form and pointing to its extinction with the decomposition of the physical form. The living ideas of past life studies move you toward wholeness. This is our greater reality, not the transitory physical body.

One needs to practice the principles of past life recall in every moment of life. One needs to become fully saturated in the spirit of these studies. One life may be too short, for even the most accomplished are yet in the midst of self awareness. Past life study is about the maturing of one's spiritual character. It requires you to treat yourself and the world in the most appreciative and reverential frame of mind. It is the study of our immortal consciousness and reincarnation heredity. It is the study of the interrelation of all interdimensional phenomena. It is the study of the Infinite plan.

Past life study is based on the first and second basic laws of physics. For every action there is an equal and opposite reaction. Therefore, if you abused in one lifetime you will be abused in the next. The second law states that a body in motion continues along its line of motion unless acted upon by an external force. Therefore, we repeat destructive life patterns unless through past life work we disrupt the continuity of soul-less life scripts. Of course we cannot say with certainty; but we can say that there is a *high probability* that something will occur again if uninterrupted. It is the principle underlying the interdimensional physics of energy.

One develops a sense of freedom when one recognizes that every cause must have an effect. Consequently, nothing appears on the body unless there is a mental pattern corresponding to it. In other words, all mental and physical conditions had their first cause in an experience from a previous lifetime. It is a past condition reinstated in the present, which has resulted in malformed psychic structures. One needs to understand this concept in order to heal all mental and physical conditions. We are interdimensional beings, a synthesis of energy fields of many different frequencies. Recognizing that we are interdimensional beings is the way toward awakening the mind which is imprisoned by unresolved chaotic energy. By understanding these patterns as originating from past lives, then you can release them. The suffering can be ended!

The terrestrial worlds are not the only worlds which exist. There are fourth-dimensional worlds extending beyond the physical body that are not limited by time and space. The psychic anatomy is a fourth-dimensional energy system that is non-atomic. The physical or atomic organism is limited to one cycle of birth and death, but the psychic anatomy cannot be destroyed. It is regenerative due to its fourth-dimensional and spiritual nature! This regeneration could not take place if the psychic anatomy did not function from a higher-dimensional energy system than the physical anatomy. It is the same energy but at a higher frequency.

The higher frequency of the psychic mind empowers the individual to attain to an interdimensional spirit. Consequently, the thrust of past life work is to open up the mind of the individual to the spiritual factors that contain the answers to all problems. Man is a regenerative evolutionary spirit. There is no death nor is there a birth; but an evolutionary development that progressively attunes the individual to the Infinite Force that is the inner and higher self, an eternal creative Infinite Force. The atomic structure of the physical body is the smallest component of this Infinite Force.

In order to cancel past life negations, one needs to take

full responsibility for one's experiences. You will develop a further sense of freedom by this acceptance. In order to develop this acceptance you will need to begin to differentiate between your physical self and your psychic self. *Your psychic self is infinite!* It is a continuous traveler. It journeys from one lifetime into another. The physical self is merely a vehicle for the psychic self. It transports the psychic self and sheds its atomic body at the end of each sojourn of third-dimensional life. When the physical self errs, the psychic self makes no judgment. Rather the psychic self learns and grows from the difficulties which the physical self experiences. These difficulties are a part of the soul's growth. Accepting both the positive and negative polarities of your interdimensional being is the process of spiritual evolution. This objectivity about our experiences is critical for full acceptance. Full acceptance is essential toward full responsibility.

Once you have gained the recognition of yourself as an Interdimensional Being and accept full responsibility for your past lives, you will provide yourself with the freedom to grow by expanding your awareness and gaining a greater perception of reality. With this knowledge your soul will unfold, and you will develop your spiritual consciousness. This unfoldment will attune you to the Infinite and allow you to live future lives on a higher spiritual frequency. You will awaken your innermost wisdom, the source of a Higher Inspiration. Then you will realize that we are all identical in spirit, in essence, and nature with Infinite Creative Intelligence. You will experience a transcendence that is revolutionary, and changes will occur in your life.

Past life work is not a case of mystifying secrecy, but rather of the understanding of science and energy. Our future depends on this understanding. Our future depends on the understanding and application of the dynamic principles of the physics of past life studies. How much negativism you cancel out from past lifetimes will depend on the course of action you take today. Past life work is not just about symptomatic reduction, but about the journey of the soul. This journey will restore choice and bring healing. You will not want to return to your previous sterile limits of ordinary physical consciousness!

Past life work supersedes any other studies for the meaning of life because an interdimensional understanding of the process of life is our connection with the "essence of life". Past life studies make us aware that we are spiritual beings, that we need to look beyond our physical bodies, and cut through the conditioned limits of time and space. Time and space are constructed by our mind. We need to see ourselves within the full framework of our multiple interdimensional lives. In this way we dance with Infinite Creative Intelligence. When we dance with Infinite Creative Intelligence we dance with ourselves.

The principles of past life studies explain the person as an energy being which is the sum and total of many lifetimes and evolutions. Man has a higher self which is his motivating life force, an abstraction of the Infinite. Man's higher self is the psychic anatomy which is the central function of each one's life. The psychic anatomy is structured from intelligent sine waves. Intelligent sine waves are life experiences. The properties of the psychic anatomy are the superconscious, mental conscious and subconscious. The psychic anatomy together activates the physical counterpart - the atomic body.

The study of past lives attunes you to the rhythms of life. It assists you in leaving one mode of existence and entering into a new and higher quality of experience. It dissolves the limitations of time and space. From your present perspective this seems extraordinary; but once your perspective becomes broadened, it will be quite natural.

Furthermore, the application of past life studies in one's life rectifies - corrects malfunctioning energy sine waves, and acts to prevent its re-occurrence in psychosomatic disorders, such as depression, obsessions, cancer, allergies, etc. Correcting these malformed structures requires you to access your past lives and find the originating cause of that problem in previous lives. To acquire these corrective measures, however, you must concentrate your thought energies. These corrective measures are instigated by your participation at all times in all aspects of your life.

The atomic genesis of man, therefore, is not the true spiritual nature of man. "Consequently," relates Dr. Charles Spiegel, Past life Psychologist, "man cannot die because he was never the physical organism. He simply inhabited it, contained it, and directed it." The beginning of life, then, is an interdimensional statement. Life does not begin in the physical or atomic dimension. The physical body is merely the laboratory in which we have our life experiences.

Consequently, when we lose our body at so called death, we do not lose consciousness of what we consider to be life. We reincarnate with other persons with whom we are harmonically connected from our past. We continue to make contact with the same individuals as long as we have mutual problems to resolve. We repeat these patterns and work through them until we achieve wholeness (our soulic nature), a more subtle wholeness than that with which we are born. We are spiritually created as a whole note. We are not an assemblage of parts. This inherent wholeness needs to be developed to the greatest degree to guard against fragmentation. The study of past life recall helps us to recover our lost wholeness and to strengthen the psyche to resist future fragmentation. The ultimate goal is psychosynthesis. We continue to experience certain problems until they are understood. *We are born again and again in order to perfect ourselves!*

Through the application of past life recall, you can learn to interpret details of your present life in a new manner. In recalling past life experiences you discharge the energy that is tied up with deep rooted memories so that they no longer create disease. You will no longer react. You will heal yourself through a transformation of energy because problems are not physical, they are psychic!

Every effort on your part opens up the window of your mind so that it becomes more than a peep hole through which the Light can shine. That is why Dr. Ernest L. Norman, Master and pioneer of Past life Therapy and co-founder of the Unarius Academy of Science has commented that, "All positive achievements are the substance of the Creative Intelligence." Every effort therefore has the potential to bring you one step closer to being in tune with the Infinite. I like to use the analogy of the light bulb. Every positive act or thought helps the light bulb shine brighter until it is all light. Every negative thought or act dims the light until it burns out and results in darkness.

Self knowledge requires persistent, deliberate effort and the highest responsibility and wisdom. As you grow to know yourself through past life studies, you will experience fewer frustrations and irritations because you will recognize the origin of situations. Your relationships with people will improve because you will understand rather than project your negativism on others. You will realize that conflicts with other people are projections of conflicts from your own past.

Past life recall, however, which does not bring into the consciousness of the individual the life of the Spirit, does not lead to growth of character. Christopher Bache, a philosopher states, "Reincarnation makes us aware that we are essentially spiritual beings and can understand ourselves only when we look beyond our physical bodies and perceive ourselves in the frame of our own histories and beyond time itself." The understanding of past lives is the only description of life that makes sense and fits the facts to explain the logic and reason of evolution!

A secret unrest gnaws
at the roots of our being.

Carl Jung

Chapter Two

HEALING

THE PHYSICS OF ENERGY

Healing is scientific. It is a change in energy. It is a change that you, and only you, can create in yourself. An intention on your part to heal yourself alters your enzymes and hemoglobin values. An intention on your part alters the chemistry and energy of your being. Consequently, health and disease do not just happen to you. They are the results of the active processes of your mind. Health is the result of a harmonious mind and disease results from the disharmony of the mind. Recognizing this carries for you implicit responsibility and opportunity. When you participate in the process of your own health, no matter how unconsciously, then you can overcome your own disease. Pierre Teilhard de Chardin stated, "The ills from which we are suffering have their seat in the foundation of human thought."

Since healing is scientific and is a change in energy, let us look at the principles of energy in order that you may understand the science of life. All matter consists of atoms. Atoms are made up of tiny particles. The universe and everything in it is matter.

There is no intelligence in matter, however, except that which has been crystallized through the Energy Source of our consciousness. Mind is the only intelligence. The body is matter. The body is made up of atoms. The body is an atom. It is an aggregation of protons and electrons. These particles are the same in every type of atom, although their numbers vary. For example, a butterfly and a person are both made of atoms. What makes one a butterfly and the other a person is the different numbers of particles inside the various atoms that combine to create them. The basic patterns are the same but different energy constitutions. The more you understand atomic energy, the more you understand yourself. However, understanding atomic energy is one thing; making use of that knowledge is another. Let's look further into atomic energy.

Atoms are made up of particles called electrons, protons and neutrons. Protons are positively charged (+) and electrons are negatively charged (-). This is the polarity component of all matter. These particles are electrically charged. The role of the neutron is to keep the atom together. Energy is the force between the positively charged nucleus and the negatively charged electrons. This interplay is responsible for all phenomena in our physical environment.

Atoms are the ultimate independent units of our being.

The more atoms are confined, the more they move around. They resist confinement. When atoms collide, the energy of the two colliding atoms creates particles which redistribute to form a new pattern. These particles live for a short time and disintegrate to again reconstitute into other subatomic particles. They are created from energy and vanish into energy. This is the transformation of energy. Energy cannot be created or destroyed, only converted from one form to another. Therefore, you as an energy body cannot be destroyed, but merely transformed. You are infinite!

Since thought is energy and energy has always existed and will continue to exist, then thoughts have always existed. As your thoughts surface, they register as a sine wave, oscillating energy throughout the body. The sine waves are characteristic of everything and are patterns of potential. We feel this shift in energy in our body. As you focus your thoughts, the atoms react to this confinement with motion and come closer and closer to the surface (awareness). The atoms become strongly excited and the frequency, (number of complete waves made in one second) increases. So now you would be functioning at a higher frequency. The higher your awareness (available information), the higher your level of frequency. At a distance (thoughts or experiences out of awareness), the atoms are more spaced out, less concentrated, less confined to one topic, they are less excited. At a distance, the force becomes strongly repulsive in order to keep the object in its stable state.

With higher energy, sine waves look like this: ∿∿ This is the appearance of a higher frequency energy wave form with more peaks and troughs. A lower frequency wave form looks like this: ⌒⌣⌒⌣

Both waves cover the same distance, but they vibrate or oscillate differently. These information sine waves forms are the energy patterns of your psychic body registered from your thoughts and emotions.

When two waves have the same frequency and direction, and peak and trough at the same time, they are said to be 'in phase'. The combined amplitude of two 'in phase' waves is larger than a single wave.

Sine waves in-phase

Resultant sine wave is the harmonic of the two sine waves, now reflecting a higher amplitude.

This means that the sine wave is carrying a lot of information energy. In physics this is called constructive interference. In the science of life, this is a unified polarity. A unified polarity carries great power, in terms of the energy they have to be able to accomplish common goals.

When 'out of phase' waves meet, they peak and trough at different times. The amplitude of their resultant wave is zero (smaller than that of the waves before they meet), as they, in fact, cancel each other's energy.

Sine waves out-of-phase

Out-of-phase sine waves cancel each other

This is called destructive interference in physics. In the science of life it is oppositional polarity.

Energy which can process information and act accordingly, can be given up by an object if it is opposed or resisted. A person can decrease their awareness (give up energy) by discounting (opposing) their thoughts. Here you disrupt the flow of current (energy) through the circuits (the mind). A break in the circuit stops current from flowing.

Energy which builds up and is not released is called static energy in physics. Once it has built up it can persist for a long period of time. An example is rubbing your feet on a wool rug on a dry day. The electric charge builds up on your feet and then suddenly it is released through your skin. You feel an electric shock. In life, certain experiences create static energy and remain in our psychic body for a long period of time until it attempts to release itself. When we have difficulty releasing this static energy or are unaware of it, we develop a physical or mental illness. The severity of the illness is in direct proportion to the number of lifetimes this static energy has been accumulating, similar to a capacitor. One needs a conductor to release the energy of one's emotions, so that it will not accumulate static charges. This conductor is past life study and application which helps you objectify and release the energy. When the energies of a negative (thought) nature are high enough to disturb the atom's (person's) equilibrium, we have a nuclear reaction, i.e. cancer, psychotic illness, etc. The agony of the spirit is reflected in bodily function.

You can see then how your evolution is concerned with every thought you think. Every thought you think is a reflection of your spirit, your higher frequency. Your mind is your spirit, which lives in a higher dimension than that of your physical anatomy and brain. Your senses are the temporal source of supply for the content of the spirit mind.

You make or unmake yourself with your thoughts. By your thoughts you either become one with Infinite Creative Intelligence or descend below unfathomed proportions. Life will be richer or poorer for the thoughts and deeds of today. Between these two polarities are all the opportunities for your psyche's spiritual evolution. You are the master, molder, maker, and shaper of your soul. You hold within yourself the transforming and regenerative power to make yourself what you will. A thought then, is like a seed; it produces whatever you plant. Therefore, you are where you are by choice. Your circumstances have grown out of your thoughts and you have attracted that which you secretly harbored. In life you attract what you are, not what you want. You get in life what you earn by your mental thoughts and physical actions, life after life!

Life then must be about spirit because Spirit is the embodiment of the Infinite Creative Intelligence. Spirit is about energy. Energy is cyclic in nature. We know from physics that energy is in ceaseless motion and change. Everything in nature, the physical world and human situations, functions through cyclic patterns. This energy is the Infinite Creative Intelligence. When you understand energy, you know of the Infinite. These understandings will help you connect to your true inner self because this is your real identity. You are an Interdimensional Being extending from the fourth dimension. When you are not connected to your inner self, your life becomes barren. You are dead to your spiritual identity. The understanding of energy principles will help you establish contact with your Spirit, with your true Brain, your true Intelligence! True healing, therefore, takes you back to the Source. Anything short of that is temporary.

You are learning about the different factors that make up what you finally can become, a spiritual being who has the ability to activate your higher senses to become clairvoyant. You are an energy body, an electronic sensing device. As it is now, you have not developed the properties of your electronic sensing device sufficiently. The psychic body, mind and spirit, your computer, is an electronic field of energy wave forms which are coupled with other electromagnetic fields. They are vortexes which contain intelligent information. These vortexes expand with the addition of more information.

Your mind has infinite intelligence. It can be nurtured. It does not need to be restricted by your five sensory body. The nurturing of the mind takes place on this earth soil. It is on this dimension where one begins to understand one's inner nature, through objective life experiences! This nurturing must include love, candidness and absolute intellectual sincerity. To do this you must become conscious of (but not lose consciousness with) your past. You have to overcome the negative blocks creating an imbalance in your life. This awareness and analysis is just a beginning of the need to reach deeper and deeper.

If you are dedicated to your progressive understanding of yourself, then in some future lifetime, these malfunctions which have caused disease, whether physical or mental, will be cancelled, resulting in an integration of body, mind and spirit. The cancellation process, of course, requires a constant honest evaluation of yourself at all times. You will need to become aware of how your negative thoughts exist and how they manipulate you.

You have the ability to objectify any imbalance in your subconscious with the recognition that the imbalance is a priority of the old self, and that the true self is the spiritual self.

The old self, or subconscious, that entertains negative

ways of life is not your true self. Therefore, you need to bring it out and cancel it. Otherwise, your thoughts will victimize you. Remember that your body will respond to your thoughts. To the extent that you can do this, your higher self will have greater energy.

Through an understanding of the physics of energy, the electromagnetic process that activates life on all levels, you can begin to touch the spiritual component of yourself, the higher frequency of energy that is your higher self. You will become all that you can be. This is not about entertainment, but about touching your spirit.

Your spiritual evolution is a continuous process. You will continuously be breaking and forming newer patterns. You will be creating new richer wholes. However, at any time that you settle for a narrow "normal" consciousness, you will regress. By admitting new information, enlarging your awareness, you will leap forward. Each time you admit new information you will be in tune with your true self, and your capacity to integrate and reconcile opposite factors of yourself. You do need a new mind for self-transformation and you need to learn a new language since language molds thought.

Your compounded life experiences, your hard disc (akashic records) live in the energy structure of your psychic (mind - spirit) anatomy. This is the chamber that holds all the reflections of your past. It is a record of all you have done. To begin to recognize particular experiences from your past lifetimes, you need to conceive of the positive factor of your higher self as it is oscillating on the spectrum of the fourth dimension. According to physics, something cannot "be there" until we can conceive it. Our knowledge is state-specific so that our fund of knowledge is dependent on the state of consciousness we are in. Each step you take in trying to apply and use this understanding develops this ability. You can do this once you gain strength through knowledge of the fundamental principles of energy. Then you can begin to add certain objective aspects of the experience to yourself. Becoming impersonal is a basic tenant of this expanded ability attained through the science of life.

Aziz-Nasafi, an Islamic-Persian mystic of the thirteenth century stated, "On the death of any living creature the spirit returns to the spiritual world, the body to the bodily world. In this however, only the bodies are subject to change. The spiritual world is one single spirit who stands like unto a light behind the bodily world and who, when any single creature comes into being, shines through it as through a window. According to the kind and size of the window less or more light enters the world. The light itself, however, remains unchanged." In reality then, incarnations exist only as a concept in a third-dimensional physical world. For the spirit there can be no past incarnations because the spirit has no past. Incarnations exist only in terms of the ego which takes itself to be somebody. When we extinguish the ego of our temporal birth, we realize consciousness is never born and never dies. Consciousness lives in the timeless present.

Wait without thought,
for you are not ready for thought.
So the darkness shall be light
and the stillness the dancing

Alan Watts

Chapter Three

MEDITATION FOR ENTERING
A PAST LIFE

Meditation is a useful tool for the beginning student of past life studies. It provides you with an experience rather than an explanation. Later you will find that insights of former life experiences will come on their own without any formal effort. The Zen Buddhists have said, "A finger is needed to point at the moon. However, once the moon is recognized, we should not trouble ourselves with the finger. It will no longer be necessary."

Meditation is a technique which aids in bringing about harmony between the psychic and the physical body. It promotes integration and helps you get beyond the body-mind duality. It triggers a recognition by breaking up old patterns. Meditation is change by a system which is safe and inner-directed. Meditation creates a new knowing by

63

activating a significant energy flow. The use of this concentrated and focused "thought energy" is often called
"psychokinesis". Meditation shifts your awareness from
the rational to the intuitive. It is the most intelligent
energy in the universe. This shift produces an extraordinary awareness and deep inner shifts begin to take place.
Meditation takes you into your interior self and develops
your psychic perceptions. Your perspectives begin to shift
sharply and you will sense the divine anchored deep within
you. Meditation helps accelerate positive evolution.

It is very important that you understand these felt shifts
or "inner knowings" which take place in meditation.
These felt shifts are the clustering of atoms resulting in
increased levels of energy which vibrate within your system. When you do not listen to this "inner voice," the
voice of your spirit, your personality cannot evolve. Thus,
disease is merely dis-ease. Disease is a state of not feeling
comfortable with yourself. When you are not in tune with
your higher self, then you are out of sync with your
spiritual essence. You become diseased and ill. A search
for yourself, therefore, is a search for your health. Knowledge of the psychodynamics of one's self can be found
through the science of life, the physics of energy.

These felt shifts are actual changes taking place in your
consciousness as a result of your mind's intentions, or your
thoughts. Your brain waves reflect the fluctuation of
energy which takes place in your body as transmitted by
the thoughts in your mind. Every human intention (every
mind activity) will result in a physical action.

Your mind is an infinite structure; it is non-atomic.
Your mind is an electromagnetic field which functions at
a higher frequency than your physical brain. The mind is
the transmitter. It transmits energy-information-sine

waves to the neurons of the brain (the receiver). Whatever is reflected through the eye and brain of a person results in a harmonic interplay with the psychic structure of that person. That is the nature of energy. You learn to see energy as the entire nature of your consciousness. Energy is you. You are an electronic system. Energy is the generic expression of your life. It cannot be destroyed. It can only be transformed. This is a basic fundamental principle of the science of life.

These 'felt shifts,' that are activated throughout the system, begin to create new connections, throw off old negative imprints, and tap into your organic memory which is maintained in the cells of your psychic body. An inward focused state in meditation creates a significant energy flow. These higher energy flows create a reorganization, since the new patterns cannot be contained in the old structure. In this transcendent state, you will defeat the misnomer of time and space because mind has a fourth-dimensional timetable. Mind is always NOW. There is no before or after for mind. Life is fluid and life is circular.

Life is an infinite process and is based on frequency and harmonics. This is the reality. These shifts will at times result in "flashbacks" to your past; yet they will be further verified by you in time. These relivings and accompanying feelings must be objectified in the present within the perspectives of changed relationships. You will experience a quickening of the spirit that is the outpouring of this process. This type of expanded conscious functioning is capable of profound change in your life!

Living matter is energy. Energy evolves to higher and higher frequencies. The mind is energy. The mind is the artist producing the whole. Since the mind is energy, it also evolves to higher and higher frequencies. This is the expanding power of the mind being utilized in meditation. Since mind and matter are alternate polarities, then death is a transition, not an end point, and the beginning of life is an interdimensional statement. This is a prototype of a different way of thinking!

Carl Jung, the Swiss psychoanalyst, drew attention to a "transcendent dimension of consciousness, the union of the psychic with the physical." He cautioned about living in straight jacket conventional assumptions because there is a dangerous blindness in accepting the prevailing view of society. When meditation expands the realm of your experience, the limitations of your rational mind will become apparent. You will modify, abandon, or transcend your existing concepts.

This process will upset your tidy little world as you emerge from your dark prison. You will awaken after years of being asleep. "One must lift one's eyes to look over the wall and must recognize that one has been imprisoned within the cave of reflected images, which one has assumed to be real," commented Dr. Charles L. Spiegel, Past Life Psychologist. If you want to grow in your spirit, you have to get beyond the fear of turbulence that too much awareness can generate. This awareness of depth which can lead one from darkness to light is there. The technique involved is the recognition of one's responsibility for past action, *the awareness that the corrective and preventive factors of life are the result of a positive catalytic agent, the Infinite Creative Intelligence!* We touch the Infinite each time we meditate.

Each individual is a stream of consciousness, continuously reconstituting and re-adapting our past lives to the present. Our mind is an invisible circuitry, an electronic umbilical cord, which links us all together interdimensionally. We need to be vitally involved in the development of the mind to become harmonically in tune with the Infinite.

When you cannot conceive of something it is difficult to be persuaded that anything is there. You either conceive it or you do not. Once you see with your eyes, however, you wonder how you missed so much before. Despite overwhelming evidence, we often stick with the old and familiar. A 'paradigm shift' is essential. We need a distinctly new way of thinking about old problems that is instructive and revolutionary. We need a paradigm shift that is scientific and predicts more accurately.

All life experiences are changed into intelligent information wave forms of energy. We call these wave forms sine waves. The sine wave is an electromagnetic energy field and is the sum and substance of all thought. Spirit is an electromagnetic flux field. It functions on a higher frequency. When your intentions and/or behaviors are positive, the sine wave is fluid, flowing, projecting positive thoughts. When your intentions and/or behaviors are negative, the sine wave is malformed. The malformation of the wave forms causes disease to the brain-body, physically and mentally, as a result of its disconnection to one's Infinite self!

Sine Wave

Positive flow

Malformed waves

This sine wave is the fingerprint of the Infinite. It is the fundamental note; and you are an expression of this fundamental note. The sine wave has a positive and a negative component and functions on two poles. Consequently, you are in constant positive to negative oscillation between these two polarities. This is how you attain intelligence. This interrelationship allows you to determine the quality of information.

The Spirit is the positive polarity of your Being, while the physical is the negative polarity of your spirit. When I say negative, I do not mean negative in that it should not be expressed. The physical is essential, because it is these atomic frequencies expressed on an earth planet which allow us to climb toward the spirit. Together the psychic and the physical make up the integrative whole of the Infinite. When you overcome negative expressions, then there will be a change in frequency between yourself and those involved. Your mind is a part of the Infinite macrocosm. It has no limitations. You are the finite expression of Infinite Intelligence!

An experience is negative if it does not put you in-tune with the Infinite. You know you are not in-tune with the Infinite because you hurt mentally and physically. There is a 'soulic' hurt. To go against your inner voice and carry it out in some physical manner is the greatest sin against yourself. It is spiritual suicide. We compromise our honor for small things. We compromise our spirit. Without spirit we have nothing.

Your spiritual development is inclusive of falls since in the falling, there is learning. You will become stronger in your determination to progress. Therefore, Principle is always in action in anything you do. The thoughts that you think are basic to the harmony you wish to develop. That is why it is important to be analytical about your thinking. This process will help you touch your spirit. An aid in facilitating the process is meditation, a method of relaxing into your deepest natural state. It is your microscope for inner exploration. In silence we hear another tune. We listen to the *Now,* to what is actually happening at the moment, outside and within ourselves. In meditation, there is no past or future. Our perceptions are cleansed; everything is infinite since the natural state of the relaxed mind is multidimensional attention.

STEP ONE

Meditate to quiet yourself and become centered. Let go of self-stressing neurophysiological activity. This inward attention will generate a larger fluctuation of energy in the brain and raise your frequency vibrational rate from beta to alpha waves. The alpha level is electromagnetic radiation and are the slower larger brain waves which will increase through meditation. Beta rhythms are small, rapid brain waves and dominate our normal waking state as can be measured on the electroencephlogram.

STEP TWO

In this meditative atmosphere do not allow any concerns to well up. Any conscious efforts here will interfere with the process of tuning-in to your mental self. Just let go. Relax your grip. Deliberately let go.

STEP THREE

Wait a minute. Breathe deeply and focus on your breathing.

STEP FOUR

A thought, word, phrase or image will come to your mind.

STEP FIVE

Think about this thought, or phrase or image. We tend to inhibit these mental activities. Do not inhibit your thoughts!

STEP SIX

If you have a rapport or affinity with this thought or image, your body will respond with a shift in your energy level or a 'feeling' will become sharpened. In other words, you will have a physical experiential effect along with an intellectual awareness. An oscillation of energy will occur which no other words or images would create. As you correlate these subjective accounts with concrete physical experiential changes along with changes in the brain's electrical rhythms which result in changes in perceptual abilities, then you no longer need speculate. You are no longer dealing with suppositions. Now you have hard facts.

STEP SEVEN

Recognize a negative issue as negative. Recognition allows you to change your perspective. Look at this situation from an impersonal, unemotional attitude, and remember that an effect must have a cause.

STEP EIGHT

This experience is a reliving from your past. Take personal responsibility for it.

STEP NINE

By a fairly elementary regime of meditation, we can

recover memories from this lifetime or a past life experience. When you relive an experience in a state of highly focused inward attention, such as in the meditative state, you will disrupt your old memory patterns. You will then capture 'new' energy by your realizations. Through this process, images from your past will begin to emerge into your consciousness.

STEP TEN

Your previous views, no matter how inconceivable at this time, are only a very small part of the whole picture. What you know now, is also a very small part of what you will know later. You cannot accomplish these great discoveries in a day and they cannot be accomplished without the supplement of the spirit. This is the missing link. These discoveries require meticulous and austere labors. However, you will finally learn to live an unanesthesized life. You must have a passionate quest for truth in order to touch your spirit, your higher frequency. Then everything you do will become a spiritual dance. You will become great only by giving attention to the little deeds of your life!

PART TWO

*The Infinite is ageless...but consciousness
is the fashioning of our mind,
To become a Spiritual Being!*

Antares

Chapter Four

THE PSYCHOLOGY OF CONSCIOUSNESS

The understanding of consciousness is the fundamental premise of past life studies, and it alone makes it possible to understand the pathological processes in our life, which are as common as they are important, and to find a place for them in the science of life. A state of consciousness is characteristically very transitory. An idea that may be conscious now, may not be conscious a moment later, although it can become so again. Ideas, however, are capable of becoming conscious at any time. The reason that many ideas do not become conscious is because some other force opposes them. Otherwise, they would become conscious. Past life studies help to remove these opposing forces.

In each individual there is a coherent organization of

mental processes. These mental processes are composed of numerous diversified and interacting systems and levels. We can talk about three terms: Superconscious, Mental Conscious, and Subconscious. In the descriptive sense they are three consciousness, but in the dynamic sense only one since they are all fourth-dimensional. In some cases this description can be ignored; but in other cases, it is indispensable. I liken these three levels of consciousness to our academic system, elementary, middle, and high school, all having a life of their own yet interconnected. Man, then is a triune being.

There are varying degrees of vitality amongst these levels of consciousness as is with our academic structure. Consciousness is a dynamic system, constantly changing, not a stable fixed thing. It is a complicated energy system, but there is no reason to believe that the energy which runs the consciousness is any different than the energy which runs the universe. Energy takes many forms - mechanical, thermal, electrical, and chemical - and is capable of being transformed from one state into another. The form of energy which operates consciousness is electronic energy. It performs its work as any other form of energy. It transfers this energy from one structure to another. Consequently, the psychic anatomy, which is non-atomic and infinite, changes from one lifetime to another as energy patterns are re-experienced and released throughout our many lifetimes. With increasing consciousness, you will experience greater individuation.

In the early 1970's a British psychiatrist, Denys Kelsey, found that "patients were remembering the time of their conception when there was no developed nervous system to retain the memories." He concluded that, "there must exist in human beings an element that is capable of functioning and recording events even in the absence of a physical body." There is a higher self that exists beyond our brain/body, our atomic being. This higher self has three components and each part is a thin slice of the total mind.

The first component is the Subconscious. It is the sum and total of memories from this lifetime. It is like the screen of a computer which can only produce one screen full (one lifetime) of information at one time. It is the surface of the mental apparatus, and the closest to our third-dimensional world. The subconscious is a substation of the mental consciousness, which is its motivating force. Our goal is to reduce it. As we reduce the Subconscious, we increase the Superconscious. They function in inverse proportion.

The subconscious cannot harbor more than a very small number of simultaneous conceptions just as the screen of a computer can only show a very limited number of bits of information at any one time from its hard disc, its memory bank. Consequently, the subconscious is a world full of restrictions and of walls blocking the way. All other information must lie in the shadow of the mental consciousness (the hard disc), withdrawn from sight.

The subconscious has many animal spirits and we need to analyze these animal spirits but not suppress them. By suppressing its negative polarity, you decrease the ability of the positive polarity for deep insights. You cut yourself off from your inner wisdom, a wisdom more profound than any formal learning or culture can provide. We need to expose and integrate the negative polarity into our personality.

The second component of the higher self is the Mental Consciousness. Nothing that has been experienced ceases to exist. The experiences of all our lives are stored in the mental consciousness. The mental consciousness is a repository of all our many life experiences, and 100% of our thoughts come from the mental consciousness. All information is stored in an electromagnetic field of energy, like the hard disc of a computer, which forms the continuity between one lifetime and another. The mental consciousness is a half-way house. It is a relay station for the superconscious, and a transformer for the subconscious. It is the seat of memory.

The mental consciousness of a highly developed person provides them with the capacity of a greater awareness. So unless the mental consciousness acknowledges the presence of a thought, it cannot be brought into awareness. Again the more highly sophisticated and developed a computer software is, the more information it can make visible on its screen. However, without the right mechanisms, its functioning is limited. The mental consciousness is a memory bank, an elaborate filing system. It functions beyond the speed of light on a higher frequency. Very strong past negative experiences will be transmitted through the gates of the mental consciousness into the subconscious. This is our opportunity to re-experience and release negative life experiences in order to change the patterning and integrate the new information into our personality.

Unfortunately, many do not use the powers they possess, stored in their mental consciousness to advance the good in their life. They keep waiting for some external power to do the work for which they are responsible. This attitude is an infantile fixation and an impoverishment of your intelligence, your mental consciousness. No knowledge is of any value unless it grows out of your mental consciousness, which is influenced by your superconscious, the link to Infinite Consciousness. Herd allegiance cuts us off from our higher self, our inner wisdom. Inasmuch as we are sheep, we negate our own energy system, our Infinite nature!

The contents of the mental conscious are always accessible to the subconscious when the need for them arises. You are able to access the memory bank of a computer once you learn to operate it. It is impossible for all the information in our memory bank, our mental consciousness, to always be in our awareness. We would be overwhelmed. But it is available when needed. An example is a phone number which is not in our awareness until we need to use it. Where is it when not in our awareness? It is in the mental consciousness, our elaborate filing system.

There is no limit to the ability of the mental consciousness other than those stemming from the individual's belief system. These abilities involve the removal of your negative unconscious beliefs that it can't be done. You are hypnotized from infancy by the culture in which you grew up. Your prime task as an adult is to dehypnotize yourself. You need to discover that the perceived world is illusory with "another reality" behind it. Much of what you think is true, is a false collective belief made difficult to check because everyone around you shares the same belief. We have such enormous potential and we stand in our own way.

The mental conscious plays an important role in the production of dreams as well. When the mental conscious and subconscious work in harmony, you feel full of vigor and life. Consciousness is then expanded and you have a new vitality to your mental and physical activity.

The third component of our higher self is the Superconscious. The superconscious is a storehouse of positive energy. The superconscious is our collective spirit. It is our Higher Self, a Spark of the Infinite. It links us with the regenerative intelligence of infinite evolution. The superconscious is our soul. It is an archetype of order, organization and gives us a sense of Oneness. To be in-tune with the Infinite requires the cooperative function of the mental conscious and subconscious circuits of the psychic anatomy.

The superconscious is the soulic nature of an individual. It only accepts the most highly polarized positive experiences of an individual. In this fourth-dimensional, enormously high frequency state of energy, disease and impurities as we know them in the third dimension are absent. Here is where the sine wave is joined to become an Infinite expression.

It is the most complete expression of the Infinite. The power and frequency here are tremendous because of the higher energy expressed!

The superconscious possesses deep wisdom and is all knowing. It has the answer to any abstract question. It knows the origin of your problems as well as their resolution. Meditation helps to prepare you with an inner readiness so that you can become quiet enough to perceive this deep source within yourself.

Understanding the continuity of consciousness reduces survival fear. You become more comfortable with your current life because you know you will have other incarnations on earth worlds. Understanding the continuity of consciousness develops the responsibility to become more attentive to life's circumstances. You are no longer a robot.

Our consciousness never grows old. It is timeless, ageless, and endless. It has the same properties of the Universal Mind, Infinite Creative Intelligence, just like a drop of water from the vast ocean has the same properties as the rest of the water in the ocean. The only difference is in volume. Our consciousness is spiritual, eternal, self-renewing and regenerative. The creative principle of the universe is consciousness, and thought is the eternal energy. Consciousness is. There is nothing outside consciousness. Express it in all its beauty and glory!

Integration of the personality requires the alignment of the superconscious, mental conscious and subconscious so that the whole of one's being is conflict free and directed toward the same end. We need to get beyond the narrow world of third-dimensional sensory perception which is the *first order of reality*. We need to grasp the *Second Order of Reality*, the reality of Consciousness, a reality of a fourth-dimensional nature, which gives meaning to the absurd patchiness of the sensory world. Our higher consciousness has a perennial wisdom not explainable by atomic sensory means. It discloses that spatio-temporal limitations of self are merely optical illusions!

*Mankind is poised midway
between the gods and the beasts.*

Plotinus

Chapter Five

POLARITY
THE DUALITY PRINCIPLE OF LIFE

Polarity is the possession of opposite properties. It is a part of the subtle constitution of man, a microcosm and a reflection of the greater macrocosm. In physics it is about the positively charged protons and negatively charged electrons, and neutrons. In the triage of consciousness, the superconsciousness is the creative positive current, the mental consciousness is the neutral, and the subconsciousness is the negative pole of creation. In psychoanalysis, Sigmund Freud viewed mental life as a whole as governed by polarities. Freud defined these polarities as being subject-object, pleasure-pain, active-passive. The Chinese spoke of the world of opposites in terms of Yin-Yang. Carl Jung described life's polarities as anima - animus, or light and shadow. In the science of life we discuss this duality in terms of positive - negative polarities. If a person is to be well-adjusted and harmoniously balanced, both sides of his polarity must be allowed to express themselves in consciousness and behavior. We seek a dynamic balance between the two sides rather than eliminating the negative totally for the positive. All life's attributes are the interplay of these forces with everything containing the seeds of this principle of duality.

You are always seeing a reflection of the alternate nature of life. Energy structures always contain a positive and a negative field. If there is a day, there must be a night; if there is a north, there must be a south; if there is up, there must be down. Although the direction may change, the kinetic energy contact is not lost. There is this bifurcation in all energy structures. These positive-negative polarities assimilate intelligence in such a way that they achieve higher frequencies in their constant movement along this pole. Even at the highest of frequency, polarity exists. Therefore, evolution, no matter at which level, is a continual association between alternate functioning. The psychic structure of our higher consciousness which is fourth-dimensional, is the complimentary positive polarity of our physical structure, our brain-body which is third-dimensional. One cannot exist without the other. It is the continuous movement between these two poles which regenerates the intelligent current of our energy system.

Each individual is a polarity in his own right. All cells are bipolar. Our bodies are a polarity as we each have hormones of the opposite sex, we each are matter and we are spirit; we have an acid-alkaline balance of the body. There are two different forces within us that represent one continuing motion: Positive and negative. This polarity of man and woman within each is the basis of all creativity.

The interrelationship between these two points
through which energy travels is the sine wave.

In working your polarity you can redo the parts of yourself you find without value. This process which cancels out the negative thoughts and behavior, helps you to reach integration. Consequently, your experiences are not open for judgment but analyses. Every experience, even the negative, is a tool toward integration. That is why negative is not negative in the traditional sense of the word, in that it should not exist. The negative component of your personality is equally as important as the positive component, in that by cancelling and integrating the lessons from the negative experiences, you develop the positive side of your being. Both areas are necessary and complementary components of your spiritual life.

Intra-polarity, then, is the best and worst that is found in a person. In order to develop integration and transformation, you need to cancel out as much of what is contained in the negative polarity. This cancellation is accomplished by decreasing manifestations of negative life experiences and developing a strong persona which counteracts these experiences. Negative life experiences, are persistent. Once you cancel out negative life experiences, they are not eliminated from consciousness. They have simply withdrawn into your mental consciousness for storage. They will remain there in a latent state as long as your life is in harmony. In times of trauma and crises, they will step in attempting expression. However, depending on how developed is the positive component of your polarity, will determine the level of balance which you will achieve. The lessons learned from the struggles of the negative polarity within an individual results in wholeness. That is why it is important that these negations are not suppressed but must become conscious and understood. If you're going to know yourself you must have full knowledge of yourself. This understanding results in maturation of the Spirit Self. The Spirit self is central to our consciousness, much as the sun is central to the solar system.

We experience polarities within relationships as well. This is inter-polarity. This is the basis for interpersonal creativity. This is biologically obvious in the sex-polarity, the union of the ovum with the sperm which results in the birth of a child. Psychically, however, this union is a oneness where each of them is reborn. Homosexuals fail to polarize this union and often suffer from a sense of never-resolved separateness. For some this is similar to a heterosexual who cannot love. For others, however, this sameness of polarity is conquered through love.

All opposites are interdependent. Their conflict is a manifestation of a constant interplay between the two sides. When we reverse roles in a relationship, that is a process toward the concept of polarity. We play many opposite roles in life. The integration of these roles; i.e. homemaker-career, passive-aggressive, male-female, are all avenues for our continued spiritual evolution. Let's look at an example. Through reincarnation heredity every person carries within, the eternal image of the opposite gender. A woman for instance carries a very definite image of man. This is an imprint from previous lives and lies fundamentally in our mental consciousness, out of our immediate awareness. This imprint establishes certain standards which will influence her choice in mate selection. This is the primary cause of attraction or aversion to someone of the opposite gender. If she is passionately attracted to a specific man, then that man has the characteristics imprinted in the psyche of the woman selecting the man. If she finds the man aversive, then the man possesses traits that are in conflict with the image imprinted through the woman's previous lives. This is why many relationships are unsatisfying because partners are selected in conflict with this imprinted image. Relationships then lack harmony and stability and have difficulty becoming synthesized opposites. We have expressed both polarities of male and female in previous lives.

Sometimes positive-negative polarities, both intra and inter, may oppose one another. Other times the positive polarity must work hard to compensate for the weakness of the negative polarity. Then again the two structures, at times, unite to form a synthesis.

Opposition occurs often and everywhere during our spiritual development. Conflict is a ubiquitous fact of life. We are batted back and forth between our inner needs and outer demands of society, between individual needs and the needs of a relationship. The important issue is whether these conflicts result in the shattering of our Self or whether they can be tolerated and endured and provide the motivation and power for creative achievement. This oppositional polarity may struggle through many lifetimes to achieve psychosynthesis.

Compensation also occurs in intra- and inter-polarities such as one organism in the body or one partner in a relationship being stressed more than the other. Then the other organism or partner takes over temporarily. The principle of compensation provides some balance or equilibrium between contrasting elements which prevents the psyche from becoming unbalanced. As we harmonize and balance polarities, health is restored.

A unified polarity, or union of opposites does occur. The negative and positive polarity can be synthesized.

This synthesis becomes a very transcendent function which leads to the formation of a balanced, integrated relationship or personality. When the union of opposites, of polarities, occurs either within an individual or within a relationship, the goal toward wholeness is facilitated. This unified polarity results in a harmonious blend and the differences are abolished or transcended.

Individuals and couples reaching a unified polarity live in strong understanding that their spiritual self is on the top side of the sine wave while the physical body is on the bottom side of the sine wave. They clearly understand

Spiritual  **Material**

the duality principle of life, the polarity of nature. They transmute life experiences which distort their thinking and put them out of tune with their spiritual self. They add more positive energy to their psychic anatomy and together they raise their frequency even higher. Their intelligence is the sum and total of the polarization of their individual energy structure. Their electromagnetic force field melds together so that they become a functioning unit. Most often a unified polarized couple have experienced many lifetimes together. In their experience together, they have become acclimated. Consequently, they can work together and generate extensive results. Together they generate extensive energy.

In order to attune ourselves toward Infinite Creative Intelligence, we must bias our movement toward the positive pole so that the negative pole can be cancelled out from a lower frequency and regenerated into a higher frequency. This regeneration results in a new derivative for an individual and within a relationship. The momentum and frequency become stronger and higher.

These positive and negative cyclic forms are expressionary forms of the sine wave highway of energy which are linked harmonically through our consciousness. Our consciousness is a polarity. The Superconscious Self is a polarized abstraction of the Infinite. The mental conscious is at a lower vibratory level than the superconscious and the subconscious is the polarity of the mental Conscious. Our physical/brain body is a lower harmonic of our psychic anatomy.

They all interrelate in a cyclic movement throughout our daily lives. There is a very logical sequence to what is taking place in this process of polarities. In the Rig-Veda, the principle is expressed in the form, "I am the two, the life force and the life material, the two at once." The basic spiritual problem of life is finding expression in a whole complex of conflicts within the polarity of nature. The conflicts between opposites is the basis of all existence. It is a conflicting harmony. We can succeed only in so far as we use these polarities as instruments of the spiritual life, of the realization of union with the Infinite, that the spirit-filled message which is contained may become conscious. Remember that man as a microcosm reflects the entire mystic energy dance of life.

The personal and individual development of our consciousness is attained through countless earth-life experiences as the individuation and personal polarizing process of self. The knowledge of these infinite expressions of polarized experiences will then be retained within the individual's higher consciousness. These polarized experiences develop the Superconscious Self. Eventually, this development will reach a certain stage or cycle and the

Superconscious Self, or Spirit Self, will become the all inclusive and dominant expressive personality within that person. In this stage you will live as a creative element that functions constructively with the Infinite; the movement from Homo sapiens to Homo spiritualis!

Where there is an open mind,
There will always be a Frontier!

Charles Spiegel

Chapter Six

DREAMS
THE IMAGES OF THE NIGHT

Dreams are a continuation of the polarized movement of our consciousness. They are thoughts pushing through from our mental consciousness operating independently of our physical senses. Dreams have meaning and symbolism and bring counsel because they convey messages to our conscious awareness. A dream is a message from yourself to yourself.

It is important that we learn to read our dreams and bring forth their answers into our waking lives, since they are the inner voices of intuition. They are often times flashbacks into our past. Dreams are the clearest expression of the mind because they are impartial, spontaneous, and have no interference from external sources.

Dreams help you reflect on the sum and substance of

your multisensory being. They dip into the past and revive old memories. Dreams are highly personal. Since you spend one third of your life span sleeping, it seems only appropriate to utilize this time maximally.

The process of interpreting dreams was one of the pillars of Jungian and Freudian analyses, theory and treatment. They both understood that dreams aid toward integration. Dreams are guides which have the potential to help you break out of grooves in which you are stuck. Dreams are energy, the constant movement of our spirit.

The Association for Research and Enlightenment, a research/educational foundation in Virginia Beach, Virginia has published numerous articles on dreams. Through the many years of dream research, A.R.E. has classified dreams into three categories. The physical dream, the mental dream, and the spiritual dream.

The physical dream focuses on somatic complaints of the individual dreamer. It tunes in the individual to health problems such as infections, ulcers, cancer, high-blood pressure, improper eating habits or the need for exercise or rest.

The mental dream relates to daily stresses of our every day environment. These issues may be career/professional issues, employment difficulties, financial concerns, or interpersonal relationships. Mental dreams include problems of daily living which are not physical in nature.

The spiritual dream is often presented to us in rich sources of color. Understanding the meaning of colors greatly enriches dream interpretation. The A.R.E. foundation has concluded from its research that color in dreams is highly correlated with attributes of character of the dreamer such as whether one is in a state of positive or negative energy, qualities of selflessness or our need and drive for success or power. Color, electromagnetic energy, induces different moods and is associated with mental and emotional relationships since color is a molecular vibration of the individual emitted from a wide spectrum of the electromagnetic energy field. Colors, furthermore, have been associated with the six chakras of the physical body. Chakras are known energy centers or control points through which one can tap higher energy vibrations.

The colors of the invisible spectrum as they appear in dreams have symbolic representations. White light is the presence of all colors and associated with abundance, while black light is its polarity and is the absence of color and symbolizes loss and at times death. Red light is the color of energy, raw physical energy. Orange light is the light of enduring strength. Yellow light symbolizes clarity of mental energy. Green light is the color of learning. Blue light is the color of healing and peacefulness. Purple light symbolizes inner and outer royalty.

Dreams commonly fall into more than one category and A.R.E. discovered another category of dreams, in their many years of research, which they classified as "visions". These "visions" are experiences of precognition, telepathy, and clairvoyance.

A precognitive dream is predictive. It is a straight forward presentation of an event which will occur. Telepathic and clairvoyant dreams enter our consciousness symbolically or factually. These dreams present more in-depth work of interpretation since it is these dreams which take us into past lives. "These vision dreams," comments A.R.E. "affect the individual to the very depths of his being."

Since these nocturnal scenarios have a very personal nature, they are a highly effective tool for past life work.

A series of dreams form a coherent picture revealing patterns of past lives. They are stored psychic energy which frequently originate from the experiences which you have had in past lives. You dream continuously, and dreams are the activities of your psyche when you are asleep. This means that you have a continuously active psyche. The psyche is always trying to heal you through dream-wisdom.

You need to stay with the images which come from your dream state in order to allow a drama to surface among the complexities of your past lives. Consequently, you need to make a conscious intention to listen to and remember your dreams.

You can focus attention on your dreams by keeping a journal and pen by your bedside. Then send a message to your mental consciousness before falling asleep of your intention to remember your dreams. Then record every thought, image, character and emotion which you remember in your dream. Do this in the middle of the night, whenever possible, or upon awakening. Remember that dreams are an ever-moving flow and interpenetrations of energies. They represent various kinds of life of all varieties, forever passing from one form to another, in a ceaseless flow of energies and appearances. Dreams are the artistic creations of our consciousness, and cut through the smoke screen of our conditioning.

Apply your analytical abilities to your dream imagery so that the patterns of your lives become more clear. Don't dismiss them as illogical because they convey vital information. Look at certain levels and components of your dreams in order to maximally benefit from them. Look first at the personal or individual associations in your dream. Who are the people in your dream? Look at the characters involved. Discuss with yourself the type of people involved in your dream image. Keep your interpretations of your dreams as close to the images as possible.

After you analyze the characters in your dream, analyze the vocabulary and language and grammar of the image messages. Look at cultural images by examining clothing, furniture, and architecture. These cultural associations do place you in a time period which can further tune you into a past life. Sharing your dreams with trusted others can contribute to understanding the significance of the images and symbols experienced in your dreams. The psyche stores these past life memories which have significant contextual meaning for you and which have been unknown to the waking mind of you, the dreamer.

Analyses of your dreams is not for their intrinsic interest but to help you in your journey toward spiritual evolution. It is a way of discovering your undiscovered self since in dreams we lay defenseless and open to inner experience. The karmic patterns you extract from dream images will give you clear clues for solutions. Oftentimes, these patterns have evolved over many thousands of lifetimes and have influenced many of your relationships.

The most trivial points of your dream are indispensable to its interpretation if you're going to understand your past lives, since dreams cut through the disguise of your waking world. Therefore, look at affect in your dream and connect it with the ideational content of your experience. Also examine the intellectual activity of your dream, as well as the achievements. Analyze the symbols of your dream and any childhood material. How old are you in your dream? Now look at the moral disposition and nature of your dream.

The hypcognic state is equally as important as your waking and sleep states. The hypcognic state is the time before sleeping or before fully awakening. During this state, there is a high level of mental relaxation, likened to the alpha state in meditation, which allows rapid visual images to enter your awareness from your mental consciousness. Pay very close attention to thoughts and psychic images in this state.

It is not unusual for some to forget their dreams. Either you have no knowledge of the dream you want to interpret or you remember mere fragments which are themselves recollected with peculiar uncertainty. They seem incoherent. Furthermore, we often think that we distort dreams in our attempt to reproduce them. However, this is untrue. There is no distortion in how your mind fills in lost segments of a dream. When some events are left undetermined by one part of your consciousness, its determination is immediately effected by another part of your consciousness. There is nothing arbitrary about this filled-in information or modification. We know this even from the studies of the physical brain that when one segment of a lobe is damaged, another lobe frequently takes over in compensation.

Forgetting certainly interferes with your efforts to utilize these images of the night for past life work. This is why it is important to understand the dynamics underlying the forgetting. Dreams are forgotten due to resistance to penetrate dream thoughts into consciousness.

This resistance persists into your waking hours in the form of doubt about the material remembered which has been allowed to come through. Consequently, you need to trust with complete certainty the most trivial element of a dream as having occurred. When any element is doubted, the psychical result is blockage so that other components and details of a dream will not be remembered. Without the attitude of complete certainty and attunement to your dreams, no matter how fragmented they initially appear, analyses will come to a standstill. Remember that your dreams are the laboratory in which a research project can take place by analyzing the component factors which are surfacing upon your life screen. The tool is the analytical process which forges a greater link to your Spirit. Your dreams must be taken seriously and recognized to be a continuity of your many life experiences.

It is important to discuss and or write down whatever occurs to you in connection with a particular dream. Doubt has an interrupting effect and creates psychical resistance. Forgetting is psychical censorship. Mental resistance, therefore, is the cause of forgetting dreams, of delays in producing dream information, and/or indistinctions of the information. We know in psychological treatment that what one resists the most, invariably carries for that person the most important of information.

You need to encourage yourself to come to terms with these disagreeable thoughts, your forgotten dreams. Waking and sleeping states are not alien to one another. Resistance is what obstructs you and not any psychical gulf between these levels of consciousness.

Practice is required with these nocturnal scenarios. You need to refrain from doubts and criticisms and remain objective. You must be persistent in remembering and analyzing your dreams as in all aspects of past life work. Your interpretation of your dreams may come fractionally, bits and pieces, throughout the days and weeks. Other times they are remembered as a whole. Dreams dreamt on the same night are parts of the whole.

There are many psychical forces interfering with your

memory of dreams. You must have strength and self-discipline to master your internal resistance. This internal resistance loses some of its power during your sleep which allows the images to come through your mental consciousness into your awareness. However, the resistance is not completely eliminated since often only fragments of a dream are remembered. Other times upon waking it is often as if no dream has occurred. Sleep reduces censorship such as the alpha state in meditation reduces censorship and allows images to fluidly enter from your consciousness. The waking state, the beta state, tends to increase censorship so that the mind eliminates in the waking state what it permitted in the sleep state. Censorship, therefore, diffuses energy thought waves. The absence of censorship, relaxation and permission, free up energy thoughts to allow for their concentration. In this concentrated state, their high frequency energy level brings them to the surface into awareness.

By analyzing your dreams which are the continuity of consciousness, you can *trans-form* what is currently in-form. By taking full responsibility for the patterns, you will release it, and un-form it, and then *re-form* the released energy for a purpose which will help you to journey closer to the Infinite Creative Intelligence. When patterns are discordant with your Spirit, the vibrational forms of the sine wave are chaotic and malfunctional. Understanding dream patterns, however, can help you psychoenergetically to heal yourself since changes in your energy field affect your overall health. The dream analyses initiates a resonant balance between body and mind. Health is a matter of balance between your physical, emotional, mental and spiritual states. Your daily actions need to be aligned with your spirit in order to prevent seeds of illness from becoming planted. Dream analyses can assist this alignment.

Dreams, like thoughts, stimulate the cells of the immune system. They either protect or they kill cells. They have the capacity to cause unmanifest energy to manifest in your life. Understanding your dreams as images of the psyche and memories of past lives can produce harmony. Therefore, the dream is a self-representation of your own psyche. They are truly symbolic statements, true representation of a psychic content of great importance.

You are organized energetically and by a consciousness of function and purpose of a fourth-dimensional nature. It is this purpose which gives your life meaning and value. This purpose helps to guide your actions. Dreams are tools for learning about your purpose and assist you in staying aligned with your spiritual Self, your higher Self. The function of dreams, then, is that through analyses of patterns you can maintain a dynamic interdimensional balance. Dreams create an energetic interchange that is powerful and significant. They connect you with your spiritual essence. Spirit is unbounded, and healing can only come from the realm of the spirit. Dreams are a tool for touching the spirit.

It is critical that you develop an objective careful interpretive approach to your dreams if you are to utilize them as guides for your present life. Objective understanding of your dreams will result in important patterns which have developed throughout many lifetimes and are stored in your psyche. At this point you need to begin to identify similar patterns or attitudes in your present characterological structure. In this way your dreams become corrective tools since now you can influence your activity. Therefore, dreams provide you with a practical advantage of an inner subjective pattern. Since the dream comes directly from your psyche, you cannot attribute it to anyone else. So what comes to you in a dream must be accepted as readily as you accept your blood pressure.

Dreams, therefore, are the rich images of the dynamic movement of your psyche as having developed and evolved through thousands of your lifetimes. Understanding your dreams will result in a progression toward conscious integration and a more comprehensive personality. These images of the night are an integral component of the spiritual dance of life. I.H. Fichte speaks of dreams and describes them "as one of the secret benefactions of the self-healing nature of the spirit."

Dreams are the mark of assistance rendered by electromagnetic forces from the depths of the mental consciousness. The same energy forces which produce every similar result in the daytime are responsible for your dreams. Dreams carry us off into another world, the world of our past lives. Dreams carry on throughout waking life and are ideas which have been attached to our consciousness. Dreams derive their material from reality and do not have the power of independent production. They are relivings of experiences which are beyond the reach of waking experience. Dreams are the superior knowledge of our remote and almost extinct past. They teach us that nothing which you once experienced or mentally possessed can ever be lost. Dream memory is extraordinarily efficient. Dreams are a part of the soul's growth and are an aspect of being on the path to self-discovery.

PART THREE

Man is born again and again,

and through the never-ending

cyclic patterns of life and death,

Each man comes to the time and place

when he meets his Creator

Face to Face!

Ernest L. Norman

Chapter Seven

DEATH
THE END OF A CYCLE

Death is a mirage. Death as an end to life is a myth. Energy cannot be destroyed; it exists in an infinite number of frequencies. It regenerates and is transformed. When the physical cycle ends with so called "death", the ultimate equalizer, your consciousness continues in the interlife, the astral plane. You "go over" or you "go on the other side". At death a cycle is concluded, but your life is not concluded. Death simply concludes the negative end of the polarity principle within the interdimensional dynamics of your life cycle. You will continue your life in the spirit within a few moments, hours, or days in an astral environment, an environment which will be familiar to you and compatible with your evolutionary state. You will have a sense of having been asleep and just awakened.

This is why we look at birth as a sleep and forgetting, while death is an awakening or a remembering. Death in the earth world is a birth in the spiritual dimension; while birth in the earth world is a death in the spiritual world.

The planet earth is only your temporary home station. It is on earth that you work out the moment to moment activities that are reflections of your past; but the Earth is not your natural home. You did not originate here. Earth is your schoolroom. Death is a "going Home". It is a transformation and transcendence in which you experience a shift in consciousness. At death you enter a fourth dimensional world which oscillates at a tremendous high frequency of energy. Here you become abundant energy.

Death is a marvelous, wondrous moment in the experience of life's grand design. A moment when one is no longer aware of and occupied with the physical consciousness of the material form; a moment of closer vision and proximity with the Infinite Creative Intelligence. Therefore an attitude of calm positiveness and serene acceptance toward a cycle's end is critical in order to release ourselves from the emotional fear of death. Death is the body's inevitable dissolution, the negative polarity of our spirit. Death is the ascension of our spirit. Through the practice of past life recall we learn to courageously embrace death.

Life and death, therefore, are not two opposing forces. They are two ends of the same pole, two ways of looking at the same force, the force of energy at different frequencies. The energy of change builds as well as dissolves as it goes through its transformative cycle. Death, therefore, is a product of the stream of change in the interdimensional cycle of life. To work for the exclusion of death is to work against life since beyond this point lies the full vision of Infinite Creative Intelligence.

We need to master the art of dying so that we don't cling to life as long as possible under the influence of narcotics and life sustaining instruments which trap an inert and useless body. These devices frustrate the transition by creating a conflict in the person. Rather, the dying person needs to practice meditation as long as possible so that consciousness can relinquish its tenacious hold on its physical existence. Meditation will aid in maintaining a soulic effort into the hour of death. The rise and fall of the breath in meditation is a constant reminder of the ebb and flow process of each moment of conscious life. The condition of consciousness at the time of death is critical since it controls afterlife and rebirth.

The last thoughts before death, the last sine waves of energy before transition, are carried into the next incarnation. These electronic imprints shape and pattern your experiences. This is why it is so important to deal with the moment of death and the last thoughts in past life therapy. Through this process the patterning carried from one lifetime to another is learned. This learning aids in transforming the negative patterns so that significant healing occurs through conscious detachment. A consciousness free from all limitations at the time of death will aid the spirit toward a higher rebirth state.

Excessive grieving by family members and friends creates a destructive interference for the dying person. This is why it is so important to understand these continuity concepts. Grief results in the oscillation of inhibiting negative energy sine waves which interfere with the oscillating positive energy sine waves which are essential for a dying person attempting to make a smooth transition. Excessive grieving also interferes for some individuals after

113

death with the ability to release themselves to complete their transition to the next state. In past life therapy many significant healings and symptom reductions have been seen in working through the process of releasement. These have been noted in many professional articles. Grieving interferes with the dying person's ability to separate his spirit from his physical anatomy by keeping him attuned to the grieving person's wavelength. Grieving thoughts keep pulling the dying person back to earth. This is oppositional polarity which interferes with the flow of current (energy) through the circuits (mind).

The sense of desperation often experienced with a person's death comes from the conditioned thinking of perishability. Perishability is the belief that man's consciousness arises from his physical body, and, consequently, vanishes with its dissolution. If we believe that we are nothing more than a sensory body, then the belief of perishability is a natural conclusion.

Past life study, however, with its psychology of consciousness and interdimensional concepts is rooted in living ideas. Living ideas are ideas of infinity, immortality and imperishability which empower. Living ideas release rather than confine consciousness in physical form. Therefore, when you understand the physics of energy and the principles of life's continuum, when death arrives you will embrace it rather than experience it as a vortex of isolation and aloneness. We need to maintain a positive consciousness when a loved one dies to aid rather than hinder the transition. It is natural and normal to miss loved ones who "go over to the other side" but excessive grieving is non-productive. When we love someone we need to be happy the person is entering into a happier world.

Death is a transit state, a rite of passage, from a physical reality to the reality of the spirit. It is a graduation into a freer happier dimension. At this time all our memories, our emotions, and patterns coalesce into a vibrational energy field and survive. At the next incarnation, the beginning of a new physical cycle, these experiences are transmitted into the new subconscious and electronically imprinted into your whole being including the cells of your body. Therefore, the potential for health or disease is carried from previous lifetimes through these electronic imprintings. Through genetic coding we pass on these memories to our children resulting in the strengths and weaknesses and addictions which we see in families. As this electronic information (intelligence by way of sine waves) is stored in your consciousness, it continues to influence future lives.

In each lifetime or incarnation, these experiences are accumulated and added to your akashic records at the moment of death. They are permanently stamped, electronically imprinted on your transmigrating psyche for your next incarnation. These past life experiences, as information energy sine waves, are retained in your master computer, your consciousness. These experiences will carry with them, as well, the unfinished business of your previous lifetimes. This explains why certain babies enter our world with severe disabilities, or why other infants enter this earth gifted. They are simply expressing the accumulated life experiences and reliving previous memories of former lifetimes.

Death is a central aspect of self-renewal. It is the essence of life, and not an existential and philosophical issue to be avoided. Death-denying attitudes result from our lack of spirituality. Death cannot be qualified within our present medical framework. Within the spiritual framework of past life work, however, the distinction can be made between a good death and a poor death. A good death results from the understanding of the vital interdimensional principles of life. A poor death is due to the fear of perishability resulting in a negatively oscillating electronic wave forms which affect one in a future incarnation.

Death is not merely the total standstill of our body-machine. It is ever possible to die in good health and choose the day and time of your death. Many advanced spiritual beings have done this. As we learn to rejoice in death, we can then readily deal with the phenomenon of death in a meaningful way. When you see your existence within a broader cosmic context by transcending your human physical condition, you will get beyond the fear of death. Birth and death, this back and forth movement, are the alpha and omega of the spiritual dance of life.

Death is truly a familiar experience to us all since different cells and organs in our bodies are constantly dying and renewing. This restoration is an adaptation to changing demands. Our consciousness also must respond to changing demands since our consciousness is very transitory and dynamic. With its dynamic nature, consciousness provides us with an unbroken continuity throughout all the cyclic changes. Once consciousness has learned all it can learn in a particular state of earth life then it sheds its atomic physical body and enters another stage of growth. Death is a progressive experience in our evolutionary cycle. "Photographers have recently been quite successful", reports Ruth Norman, co-founder of the Unarius Academy, "in filming people leaving the body, as well as those who have temporarily completed the separation process. These souls on the inner", she continues, "show up on film as fuzzy, luminous balls of elongated lights. They have been photographed in motion radiating their life force". We are energy beings, first, last, and always!

Transition, of which death is a part, is a constant fact of life. Life is a process of change. Death facilitates this change. Consequently, there is no finer tribute which you can give a deceased person, than to celebrate all that was nurtured and strong in the lifetime which he recently left. This celebration expresses your awareness of the continuity of consciousness, the presence of the loved one's spirit. This process better assists the deceased for the life journey after death.

Death, therefore, is an ascension, the ascension of the spirit from the captivity of the physical form. Death is a metamorphosis, a regenerative evolutionary process. It is a change from atomic form to an energy body of light. You are an indestructible energy body. Death is merely a change in frequency. Soulic spirit energy, for example, oscillates at millions and millions of megahertz per second in comparison to human thought which oscillates only at hundreds of megahertz per second contrasted with home electrical energy which oscillates at 60 cycles per second.

Death is an integral component of a series of experiences which are never ending. We are a part of an energy system related and connected by this manner of energy. This vital interdimensional principle of life connects us all and creates our oneness.

Your perception of life then is your intelligence regenerated life after life and forming your present consciousness. Therefore, intelligence is inherited from incarnation heredity. Consequently, there is no such thing as someone more intelligent or less intelligent but only individuals at different evolutionary stages. Individuals with "high" intelligence are merely old souls who have incarnated thousands of lifetimes. They've been around the mill a few times so to speak.

Lifetimes are chosen, just as we choose a college for our studies. We are all at different levels of spiritual development as we are at different levels of academic development. We must choose the "school" best suited to our immediate needs, the "school" which carries in it our area of special interest. We then "major" in this area of special interest. We put into it our energy until we master it. Once we master it by showing scholarship in this area, we go on to something new. We choose our lifetimes, our illnesses and all our circumstances, before incarnation, in order to grow. If one chooses to consider himself an innocent victim of his environment, it is simply because he lacks a depth of understanding.

Our spirit moves into the womb and enters into a new lifetime. A lifetime is chosen simply because there is a lesson to be learned in that country, in that race, in that family or setting and with those inner casts of characters, those persons with whom we were associated in previous lifetime experiences. Every incarnation is an opportunity. We re-enter into the environment which gives us the needed lesson. Through past life therapy a person can determine if that lesson has been learned.

Self-conclusion (suicide), asisted suicide, or abortion therefore, need to be given serious reflection since they may interfere with the evolutionary process and purpose of the person's life cycle robbing the spirit of its essential vehicle, its atomic body, for carrying out its moment-to-moment daily activities. However, even in these instances one must listen to one's inner voice since no one has a right to be someone else's judge or jury and determine whether any experience enhances or detracts from one's spiritual development.

Some spirits incarnate only for hours or days in the womb or after birth. Their deaths are due to conditions of the spiritual entity in its desire to incarnate to the earth world. These spirits are affected by the negative conditions of the past life on earth. Their brief sojourn is due to an improper frequency hook-up with the new parents and therefore the birth of the spirit entity is miscarried in the womb of the mother. This condition is an aborted birth to a new incarnation of the earth plane. It is a challenge for the parents toward further growth. In other words, certain incarnations are planned for the benefit of others. Every thought, every action, every incarnation, every death is designed for the growth of the spirit. Consequently, these spiritual forces project embryonic implantation for karmic need and spiritual evolution. Contemplating parents, therefore, need to consider the high ideal involved with conception. Conception is the fertile seedbed for spirit re-entry and development.

Rebirth does not occur immediately after death. We go through a period of fourth-dimensional rest between incarnations. During this rest period we assimilate the harvests of life experiences. After this assimilation process we return to the third-dimensional world invigorated for a new adventure in learning. There comes a time when we no longer incarnate on earth for personal learned experiences. Our own earthly education is completed.

However, we may choose to incarnate to teach, to lead, to inspire by choosing various polarized roles. These roles are specifically chosen for the purpose of teaching others to learn to grow spiritually. Consequently, when someone crosses the path of such evolved spirits, it provides them an opportunity toward their ultimate achievement. We touch one another's lives for a reason. Nothing happens by accident. When we choose not to incarnate, then we remain in the inner worlds, growing in knowledge of the Infinite on another frequency and expanding our awareness of the spiritual dance of Life!

What the caterpiller calls
the end of life
The Master calls a butterfly!

Richard Bach

Chapter Eight

THE METAMORPHOSIS OF THE SPIRIT

The transition into the 'after-life' is similar to the transition of the caterpillar, which is earthbound, into the butterfly stage, an unbounded state. Therefore, death initiates a metamorphosis. It is a journey to a new city in another dimension of life where one has an endless involvement with limitless others. It is a shedding of the skin which has been occluding the energy of the inner self. Once the caterpillar sheds its skin, the butterfly is liberated.

Aggregate examples of out-of-body experiences report that the spirit which has recently vacated the body has infinite capabilities with no barriers. The spirit's bodily functions, although similar to the functions of the third dimension, are now intensified. The spirit, which has been

123

released from the physical atomic body, vibrates at a higher frequency in its isotopic state. The original atom comprising the atomic body is the negative polarity of the isotope which is the higher intelligent atom remaining after the shedding of the physical atom. The isotopic atom vibrates at a higher rate and has a different weight than the physical atom.

A historical example of life-after-death was reported by Dr. Carl Gustav Jung, a Swiss psychoanalyst. After a heart attack he was in a state of semi-consciousness. He reports having "exited my body and found myself floating away from earth in a glorious blue light and later standing before a temple, the door of which was surrounded by a wreath of flames. It is impossible," he stated, "to convey the beauty and intensity of emotion during these visions. They were the most tremendous things I have ever experienced. I can describe the experience as only ecstasy of a contemporal state in which the present, past, and future are one."

In November of 1990, I personally experienced the circle from which the Infinite radiates. This moment of ecstasy created a profound effect upon my beliefs and life purpose. It was an apocalyptic inner event. It eventually led me to further explore the interdimensional concepts of the life cycle since the experience left me longing for its essence.

I was in the office of a friend visiting with him out of state when suddenly the surroundings faded out of sight and out of consciousness. I was then immersed into a vortex of Light of a very different frequency vibration. I was totally suspended in this state. I don't know how long I was suspended in this state as there was no sense of time and space in this Light experience. I wanted to stay in this Light world. In this vortex of Light I felt totally whole, complete, and needed nothing! I experienced a heightened sense of perception since it transported me beyond the restrictions of my limited self-concept to a connection with something greater than my third dimensional self. I would never think of myself as completely separate again! This was the highest kind of state that I could possibly conceive and live. The peacefulness and sense of integration were beyond description. I instantaneously adapted and did not want to leave. Yet, I felt myself being returned to the earth world. I resisted and objected. Yet, I was returned with my expanded Self funnelled back into a constricted unit.

Since then, my frequency vibration was much higher, I felt detached and displaced in the earth world. I wept profusely for an hour for the loss of the Light world. These tears were the tears of spiritual opening.

Saint Teresa of Avila described her connection with the divine during a mystical experience: "The pain was so sharp that I moaned but the delight of this tremendous pain is so overwhelming that one cannot wish it to leave one, nor is the soul any longer satisfied with anything less than God. It is a spiritual, not bodily pain, although the body has some part, even a considerable part, in it. It is an exchange of courtesies between the soul and God."

I became overwhelmed with the meaninglessness of our materialistic civilization and the emptiness of our ritualistic activities. I felt transformed by this transcendent energy. Nothing on this earth has ever had the same significance. This moment of ecstasy was a taste of the heavenly inner realms. I mourned for weeks the loss of the inner world. I continued to feel detached from the earth world, still oscillating at a higher frequency, and viewed earth life from afar as if moving on a screen and feeling separate from it.

I have felt the reality of my inner spiritual nature, and the knowledge that I must live my life, by giving of the self, in my sojourn on Earth. Through this experience I am more aware of how the mind can function, and that spiritual insights come from the depth of our higher consciousness. As I objectified this experience of transcendency and I reestablished myself in an oscillating manner more common to the earth world, the sense of loss diminished to a great extent. I began to feel a sense of unity and interconnectedness with all of creation interdimensionally. This process, however, took several weeks before my earth life became more positively biased. This experience has produced a very rapid qualitative shift, a lasting change in consciousness itself, altering the perception of myself and the world filling me with peace, mental clarity and serenity. Experience, however, is the reality. These words are a mere shadow. Everything now is colored with a different paint brush, the brush of my experience with the Light world. The memory of the rapture of such a numinous experience still remains. Since then, I have learned and understood that the Light is not somewhere else. It is within me. This Light constituted but a narrow portion of a vast, continuous electromagnetic spectrum. I continuously carry with me this inner treasure, a treasure with which I focus all my energies to obtain and to hold - a treasure which one needs to share with people.

> Is it not the Principle of life's continuity
> to know of Infinity
> the Immortality of our Spirit,
> to so become attuned with
> the higher note of the Cosmic Mind?

Yes, we are one in Spirit,
   joined at this time and
at this junction in our life
   to overcome past life negation;
thus to make ourselves whole
   in balance with Infinite Intelligence!

You have come to me
   from out of Infinity's Warp and Woof,
to fashion a Garment created from
   lustrous colors of sparkling Energy!

Thus are we woven from the light and love
   of our Soulic Essence,
to learn from Life's Forge
   lessons of humility and the Reality of Spirit!

As you have come to me
   so have I come to you,
to touch your Heart
   and hold you close and feel
the Pulse of your Soulic Essence!

                       Antares

Later on in his evolution, Dr. Carl Gustav Jung commented that "Life after death represents another stage in the individuation of the psyche. Psychic life goes on after physical death because the psyche has not attained self-realization." Spiritual development then, is never completely achieved. Our progression is a continuous process since our environment and experience change continuously. Even in the after-life we must learn to become infinitely biased.

Life after death then is a metamorphosis which changes an emotional being into a Spiritual being. The spirit continues uninterrupted and outlives the physical body. The deathless spirit is man's spiritual immortality.

Returning Home is the most marvelous of the spirit's heroic journeys. Furthermore, this journey is inevitable. The spirit which resides in the center of the highest division of our consciousness radiates its energies into the lower worlds. As it sheds its lower self and disengages from its previous incarnation, it enters the higher plane for review, renewal and integration of all the highest aspiration it had on earth. Through the natural cycle of cause and effect, life in the higher worlds is a condition of effects caused by experiences set in motion on earth. This is the unerring, equitable, intelligent law of karma which adjusts effect to its cause and institutes them in cycles beyond time and space in whatever energy wave forms we are so concerned.

Therefore, the experience in the higher worlds is unique to every individual. You will enter a world which is familiar to you. Although the higher world will be different in terms of frequency and harmonics, you will transcend into one of the dimensional planes congruent with your evolutionary state. There are thousands of dimensional planes in the higher worlds comparable to our many universities in our earth world. These dimensional planes in the higher worlds are our spiritual universities. Your level of preparation on earth will determine the level of admission into the spiritual universities. Your evolutionary need will also determine the spiritual university which you can enter.

Saint Teresa of Avila in her most famous guidebook of

the spiritual journey *The Interior Castle* related that there are seven teaching centers or universities in the higher astral and Celestial worlds. Mohammed was guided by the Archangel Gabriel into these seven spiritual Teaching Centers. Other Cosmic visionaries Raphiel, Michiel, Uriel and Muriel have named them: Leadership, Teaching, Philosophy, Art, Devotion, Healing and Science Centers. These teaching centers are strictly based on a particular mental function in regard to the people who go there, who have evolved to that level of frequency. Each Center teaches the student advanced concepts of the reality of consciousness as a dynamic interdimensional relationship with the Infinite Cosmic Intelligence. Consciousness is the doorway to these spiritual universities. These spiritual universities are tailored to our individual differences. We are different because we are at different levels of spiritual awareness. In these universities we learn to face ourselves and the negative frequencies which blocked us in the past. However, this change will not happen rapidly in our consciousness. We all learn according to our ability to absorb a new concept. We learn at different rates of comprehension. Some require time to absorb a new concept while others have a more infinite mind pattern attained through life experience. Through these scholastic teachings we will learn to cancel out negative energy wave forms in order to be reinstated in a healthier position in our next incarnation.

Since we are all constructed of Sparks of the Infinite Creative Intelligence, the electromagnetic energy field, then it is important to realize that in the higher worlds we are being assisted by Higher Beings to integrate all the knowledge we learn at the spiritual universities. All interdimensional life forms live in cohabitation, members of

129

different interdimensional societies interrelate with one another. This interrelation of interdimensional life forms is for the purpose of transmitting higher fourth dimensional intelligence to individuals on the earth world who are just initiating their journey toward the understanding of the continuity of consciousness. Some have experienced this interconnectedness between third and fourth-dimensional world through near-death-experiences and past life recall. This is possible because the individual spirit has an interdimensional reality, which is heightened in the awareness of one's spiritual consciousness.

These higher worlds, or non-atomic spiritual galaxies, are far removed from the Earth world in spiritual frequency, where you will live, study, and learn to further your evolution. Here you will find knowledge which will be an extension of your physical consciousness. One does not lose one's individualization in the higher worlds. One's attitude and state of consciousness in the earth world will continue in the higher worlds in a similar way. One realizes one's mental nature and is more aware of one's mind with a greater degree of integration. Those who do not have an understanding of the continuity of consciousness will not realize they have made the transition into the astral worlds. They will think they have just awakened from their usual daily sleep. You will not achieve a higher state of consciousness in the astral worlds different than the one which you now can conceive.

Therefore, the astral world experience will be a continuation of your present earth life at your present evolutionary state. It could not be any other way any more than you would take a preschooler and immerse him in a high school setting on earth. It would be overwhelming and nonadaptable. It would be contrary to Infinite principles since the Infinite Creative Intelligence does not sabotage nor destroy His own "creations".

Everything we see here on earth is a mirror image of the astral worlds - homes, gardens, animal life, flowers, children and adults. All of it was fashioned there and reflected onto the earth plane. So our earth experiences are shadows of the World of Light, a plane in which you will be suffused with brilliant light and happiness, where love is the core of understanding, and wisdom transcends knowledge!

"We live most of the time in the spiritual world. The transmissions of life are instigated from the spiritual side of man's nature and not in some supposedly immediate superficial reactionary combination of conditions which might arise on the surface of his daily life," relates Dr. Ernest Norman.

In this world of Light, you can transport yourself anywhere within seconds. Travel occurs at the speed of thought, instantaneously. Spirit can read all thoughts. The language in the higher worlds is a universal language of thought projection, and not verbal speech as we know it on earth. In this brilliantly lighted environment of other beings, you will see many individuals who ascended before you whom you knew on the physical plane.

Thoughts, as we understand them, are transmitted from the psychic anatomy into our physical body. Thoughts can be considered to be interwoven in the texture of one's previous life experiences. Present life experiences shape the nature of the energy, positively or negatively with respect to how these experiences were conceived. However, our Higher Consciousness is created from a fourth-dimensional electromagnetic field where all positive concepts of life have been conceived. The frequency difference between the earth world and the super celestial world is immense, however. Consequently, we do need a way to move from the earth plane into the super celestial worlds. This intermediate world is the terrestrial plane. The terrestrial is the plane wherein all people work-out their past negative life experiences. The next step in their evolution will be lived purely from the mental state in a higher astral plane. The astral plane is not to be confused with the super celestial plane where one is totally liberated through having achieved full union with Infinite Creative Intelligence and passes beyond the human stage forever. The astral plane is where most of us reside between incarnations.

Life in the higher worlds is the continuity of life with a different paradigm with that much more integration of the Mind. The psychic structures have to be reconstituted and regenerated and this may take hundreds of thousands or millions of years so they can be able to readapt themselves to return to earth and add new knowledge. Through past life studies and recall you can initiate corrective and preventive techniques of removal of lower frequencies so that the psychic anatomy can be reconstituted so that you may evolve to a higher state of consciousness on a higher spiritual world.

On the inner planes you have not attained perfection either. Ego can get in the way even in the higher worlds. Even here you can "fall" and accumulate negative karma which has to be corrected and removed in order to reach a higher frequency. However, no failure on either dimension is final. We have endless opportunities to become what we aspire to be, a spiritual Being!

What happens, however, to those individuals who in their earth life have been significantly destructively inclined, the incorrigibles and the criminals of this world? Such personages have interfered with the equilibrium of their life. To maintain an equilibrium we need to eliminate the words good and evil, which imply a judgment, from our consciousness and replace them with the realistic concepts of physics of positive and negative energy wave forms.

"Evilness" disrupts frequency patterns of various energy formations thus interfering with the continued development of the superconsciousness. Every individual is merely expressing the common dynamics of energy transmissions. Therefore, "evilness" is the expression of a person's negative polarity with the more positive biased Infinite Creative Intelligence. Therefore, for the spiritual worlds, the "evil doer" will not have the capability to absorb spiritual energies directly into his psychic body. It is likened to a person in the earth world developing pneumonia and becoming incapable of taking in oxygen freely into his lungs. In the spiritual world he will find himself incapable of taking in freely spiritual "oxygen". However, since he needs to "breathe" some energy, he will translate to a spiritual plane compatible with the frequency of his psychic anatomy.

This compatible world will be in the lower astral or subastral plane. A destructively inclined individual will not find positive energy in his spiritual world to assist the healing of his psychic body into a higher elevation. Such a person, however, can 'turn around' the compression and degeneration of his Superconsciousness and change the course of his evolution by constructing a positive force of action, opposing the destructive act which he had performed. This process of regeneration will require many aggregate lifetimes of constructively biased acts. In this new process, the destructively inclined individual will begin to expand his contracting consciousness. There will be an extended delay in his metamorphosis, but eventually he will change from the caterpillar-like materially-bounded life to the unbounded, liberated butterfly.

The Spirit's evolutionary function when it goes through its metamorphosis is to engage in elaborate mental plans to be carried out on earth. The earth state, therefore, is not the scene of action. The scene of action is in the higher worlds on the mental plane. Man's most sublime achievements on earth come from the mental effort from the inner plane of the spirit. Therefore, earthly accomplishments are reflections of inner plane activities.

In the higher channels of expression you will have a body of a different frequency. Although it will appear similar to the one you presently have, it will not have the constituent atomic matter and skeletal mass. It will be an energy body, the psychic anatomy, an electronic energy system like a holographic image.

Our spirit then is the true symphony of life, the true spiritual dance of life. Spirituality cuts across time periods so that following fads is a great way to get outdated. So when you marry the spirit of the time, you will soon become a widow. And so the Superconscious, the "Father within" continues to guide us in our dance through the Heavens. Our consciousness continues, and so continues the journey of the Spirit in its return home.

> A story of evolution,
>   an epic song of Creation,
> a saga of enduring Love
>   beyond the limits of earthly sorrows.
> This, then is the Alpha and Omega,
>   the Pulse of Creation!

You are my Love,
   the Wellspring of the Infinite
demonstrating Spirit.
   The sum and substance for life's Passion
is to know of reality and the silence of Infinity.

                                        Antares

A reasonable soul cannot be

    without love while it is in this life...

For to love and be loved

    is the secret business of all human life.

Richard Rolle

Chapter Nine

LOVE AS AN

INTERDIMENSIONAL LUBRICANT

Love is the pragmatic fiber of life. It is the reflection of the instinct of life and is indispensable to every human being. Love is the perfected regeneration of Infinity and touches the very core of all things. When we use this recreative force within our life, we will move along the lifeline of progressive intelligence. Our essence is love. It is a natural state achieved as we reprogram and cancel past life negations. Love heals the mind and body in its continuous oscillation between its positive and negative polarity. Every act of love releases blocked energy in the atoms of our body. Love transforms.

Rollo May, a psychoanalyst, defined love as an "opening of ourselves to the negative as well as the positive ... an

intensity of consciousness we did not know was possible."
This is possible through love's indiscriminate nature. It
knows no barriers of race, age, time or space. It penetrates
interdimensionally. We live in spiritual frequency when
we transcend multiple differences as we learn that differences are not deficiencies. We fall back on our spiritual
development when we do not transcend these differences.

Love, consequently, must be a communion of consciousness since mind is one. Division easily leads to conformity
and leads to limitations and contradictions. Love is, by its
very nature, an inclusive way of life. To be inclusive we
need to get beyond the point of being satiated with ourselves and turn our focus outward in the service of human
life. We must move ourselves from being a passive vessel
to a living spring, from being parasites upon life to becoming patrons of life through our interrelatedness.

Physics itself has taught us that the universe can only
be understood in terms of relatedness. Therefore things
are nothing in isolation and atoms transform only in
relatedness to other atoms. A lone atom is meaningless
and only in relationship with other atoms does it become
the building stones of nature. Only in relationship with
other human beings do we become builders of life. Our
words and deeds stamp themselves interdimensionally.
The mansion of our soul is built out of the bricks of
relationships provided by others for our use. This is why
love always finds itself in one lifetime after another, to
reestablish its Oneness.

Love is a frequency. That frequency changes based on
our thoughts and our behavior. The incongruent is that
since we are living from our past we shape our world
accordingly. We live as reactors of prior lifetimes when
we live in ignorance of the universal interdimensional

concepts of science. It is not enough to have knowledge of progressive evolution, but we need to have knowledge of regressive evolution in order to help us grow spiritually. The core of life is spiritual. We return to earth repeatedly in order to bring ourselves into perfect alignment with the Infinite. This is the perennial philosophy of our existence. As we eliminate past life negations from our subconscious, our mental consciousness will attune itself with the super-consciousness bringing us one step closer to the Infinite. Until these spiritual truths become a part of us, our incarnations will be lost to our awareness. Through the understandings of the physics of energy, however, we will be able to recall many past lives which will in turn reveal these truths to our consciousness, converted into action. Therefore a thought is all that is needed to cause one to fall back or convert one's frequency. We either love, or we perish! The glory of life consists in our ability to feel deeply and experience widely.

Love provides the libido for living and widens our consciousness. Without love the life that we lead in any lifetime has very little meaning. We achieve degrees, we have good jobs, and we become financially comfortable. We do this for the rest of our lives like automatons until we die. Recalling, however, that life is based on polarities and all behaviors contain their opposites, then if we want to be successful and prosperous, we need to be generous!

Love is the rationality and logic of our clearest human thought reflected in selfless service to all without prejudice. In all ways love makes life worth living because it keeps you positively biased. This makes possible for the regeneration and rejuvenation of the spiritual and physical anatomy. Love is a lubricant because without love one has despair, low self-esteem and poor health. Furthermore, a person with such symptomotology cannot be a good help to his fellowman. Through love, however, he becomes a healthier person, society profits from him and he adds to the common wheel of society.

Love is the source of our consciousness and penetrates interdimensionally. In the thousands of reports documented of near-death experiences, the message has been clear, and the message has been consistent: Love is what matters! This message has been sent to us from the fourth dimensional world. Every act of love helps us step-up our consciousness into a higher frequency. In order to achieve this step-up, we need to die to our past. We need to understand that everything we do in the present is a result of past experience and that now is the passageway of our past to our future. Each time we cancel the negative frequency of past lives we prepare ourselves for the next step-up in consciousness.

There is a price to be paid, however, for every step-up in consciousness. You cannot be more sensitive to love without being more sensitive to pain and danger. This susceptibility is the soil for further spiritual growth. As your frequency increases, you will develop less interest in what the finite, physical, material world has to offer. You will develop a greater awareness that you are not of this world even though you live in it. You will know that your heart and soul are made not for the finite but for infinity. The discontent of your soul while in the third-dimensional world is the sign and seal of its infinity and divinity.

Yet the criterion, Love in action, can only be manifested when we learn to Love ourselves, the True Self, which is Spirit incarnate. This means to "Know of Self," within the Alpha and Omega - the interdimensional matrix of the microcosm and the macrocosm. The principle of

Love, then has a greater meaning as an evolutionary design of the soulic purpose through life experience. Love will then be an inner expression which radiates the power of Spirit, the higher note of the Infinite Creative Intelligence.

So the basic criterion of spirituality must be understood. It is an evolutionary perfection of love and compassion. It is an intellectual perfection of wisdom and knowledge of interdimensional spiritual concepts. Spiritual evolution involves a genuine development of love and a willingness to put that love into action for the service of others. How quickly the world can be regenerated if we give all to love. Love is the essential lubricant of the soul. So pour this anointing oil on the relationships of your daily lives.

Love was inspired by an immortal hope, but it requires mortal effort and action to keep it alive. We do this by turning our allegiance from self to mankind as a whole. In this way we transcend ourselves and become a link in the electromagnetic force of humanity. An individual who has linked himself by chains of love with all the Master Builders of our interdimensional civilization by leaping over space and ignoring time is truly performing the spiritual dance of life to a tune of an unforgettable symphony.

The polarity of love is fear. This polarity is ontologically necessary. Love and fear are inseparable and always present in oscillation just as the systolic and diastolic of our heart-beats echo this polarity in the universe. The polarity of love, just as the polarity of our pulsating blood stream, is a reflection of the continuous rhythm of every moment of our existence.

Fear is an energy current in our body. It is an insidious power and very tenacious. It is produced by a psyche cut off from its Source. It is the absence of a sense of being loved. It keeps an individual self-centered, wastes useful energy, and is the cause of all impairment. Jesus understood this and knew that it could be eliminated. He constantly reminded us to "Fear not, be not afraid." A person who is threatened from the inside has a nagging concern to secure himself because he feels in a constant state of existential alienation. In this concern, he closes his heart and has little interest in another except as the person threatens or promotes his own end. A person under the imperious influence of fear can never see others as people in their own right because he is like a ball of string, he has difficulty disentangling himself. Since we are members of society, one of another, fear can never be a private affair. It serves as an obstacle to the individual's positive consciousness and alienates him from the Infinite since a fearful person's overriding goal is to keep his emotional economy undisturbed. He resonates his pain throughout the entire universe as he turn upon himself creating an illusion of separateness and dualism resulting in a prison of individuality and preventing him from wholeness. A fearful person's field of awareness becomes significantly narrowed. He will include in his awareness what relates to his emotional needs. Everything else is excluded. A fearful person is not an evil person, however, evilness is the absence of goodness. What does exist is a forgetting of one's greatness. A fearful person forgets to turn on the Light. The Hitlers of this world are buried in this forgetfulness.

A person in fear has biochemistry which is unbalanced resulting in distorted viewing because he sees with his moods. It steps down his vibratory level reaching the lowest pole of negativity in the physical universe. In this handicap, he becomes obtuse creating tension in every relationship. Fear is reflected outwards into interpersonal relationships. Such impoverishment had its first causation in an experience incurred in some remote and previous lifetime. The objective then is to rectify the malformed energy structures in the psychic body by going back clairvoyantly into your past lives to find the basic cause for the absence of love which was the originating source of trouble. Then we need to live each moment of consciousness with our feedback connected, with the knowledge of the resurgent past life patterns. We will relive our past numerous times until we cancel the negative frequency patterns by applying the physics of energy until it results in our healing. Spirituality, then, is each one of us undefined by fear, and integrated with our higher intelligence!

A person infected by fear infects others and sees everything in terms of "I need" because he is turned inward upon himself. This increases his isolation from others which eventually leads to self-alienation. He cannot escape unaided from this quicksand. In fear a person leaves undone what ought to be done and does what he needs not to be doing. Fear is regressive and degenerative. Do not dance with fear. Dance with love which is the companion of Light!

Harry Stack Sullivan, a world renowned psychiatrist, defined love: "When the satisfaction or security of another person becomes as significant to one as in one's own satisfaction or security." Love then is the active concern for the growth of the person whom you love. The needs of that person become as important as your own. Love helps others realize themselves by providing opportunities. It is progressive. It is not demanding. Pressuring people to do what one wants them to do does not lead toward an expansion of consciousness. Pressure, clutching, and possession diminish one's spiritual energy. Even if a person does what one wants him to do, that person will cringe inwardly. The victory, furthermore, is actually a failure because it interferes and blocks the other person's karmic process. Such processes need to unfold on their own.

We must develop an inner tolerance for the essence and uniqueness of others. Love, therefore, requires a letting go of private imperialism, the need to conquer individuals nearest and dearest to us. Tolerance preserves; it does not destroy. A letting go is pure love. We need to love without coercion, without taking credit, and in a nourishing manner. Based on the polarity principle, an over-determined behavior produces its opposite. Persons eternally seeking power are lonely and naked in a world that has never woven a garment of love for them. They have relentlessly driven themselves into a spiritual vacuum.

A loving person can stand back once a process has been energized and formed. Since love is not to be laden with expectations, no outcome can be a failure. A person with no expectations of another is a person at peace. A person at peace is to be respected. This inner peace passes on to others and transcends understanding.

Love cannot be bought through money or pleasures. It is not possessive. It is not licentious, doing what you want, but requires discipline. It is a gift which comes from the pureness of one's heart. It comes from the quietude of one's consciousness. In life love is all that matters.

Love is Spirit incarnate. It is Love in Action. It demonstrates itself in one's total acceptance of other people in an objective manner, by not judging them and by letting one's frequency and basic nature be felt by another. The capacity to love others is intimately tied up with the experience of being on reasonably good terms with oneself. When one is in good terms with himself, he will manifest an increase in spontaneous good will toward others.

Automatons cannot love. They merely exchange their

personality packages and hope for a fair bargain. On the other hand, love is not the absence of conflict. Destructive interchanges do create division. However, conflicts experienced at a deep level of inner reality lead to clarifications. Here both individuals emerge with a greater awareness, knowledge, and strength. The aliveness and strength which develops after such an interchange is the proof for the presence of love. When we do not flee from ourselves and become one with ourselves, then we become one with each other.

Love is not an exceptional-individual phenomenon. It is a state of absolute and unconfined frequency of energy accessible to every one in the midst of every experience. The drive to love the world is an inevitable facet of our spiritual maturation. Love must be experienced not in thought, but in the act, in the experience of oneness. Love in action, therefore, is the predominant proof of an individual's understanding of interdimensional physics; understanding of the reality of life and death; and understanding of the importance of changing negative biases, which are the functioning basis of the subconscious, by changing the falsity of a particular belief.

Love is an interdimensional bridge. It is the root of our creative spirit which relates us to the unbounded Spirit. Without love we are stuck in the quicksand.

Love is an action in the mood of eternity, interdimensionally, rather than that of linear time. It is a Spiritual Current and lives in a timeless realm. In every act of love we mold ourselves. This is love's dance with Itself.

Meditate on love. With every inhalation take in love; with every exhalation expel fear. Love is our lifeline. It is transspatial and transtemporal. It is the Divine Within!

PART FOUR

I can give you nothing
        that has not already its
being within yourself.
        I can throw open to you
no picture gallery but
        your own.
I help you to make
        your own world visible.
That is all.

Herman Hesse

Chapter Ten

CASE STUDIES
IN PAST LIFE THERAPY

All somatic disturbances contain deeply repressed feelings from a past life trauma. The body responds to every thought which we carry within ourselves. To access the repressed traumas, it is essential that sensate consciousness is focused on the area of disturbance. Past life traumas are deeply imprinted on the body. By focusing on the somatic element, the hologram of a trauma can be accessed for therapeutic processing. It acts as a bridge to the past life experience.

Case I - A Case of Unresolved Grief

When Joni came to see me she was a very successful business executive with an income in the six-figure range. She consulted me specifically to overcome a physical problem.

In general her life was in order, but she found the debili-
tating pain in her knees distracting although she never
allowed the pain to interfere with anything she wanted to
accomplish. I used her symptoms as the ingredients for
the induction to gain entrance into her past life which was
resulting in this unresolved experience. I asked Joni to go
to the event responsible for her knee problem. One
induction proved to be enough to tap into the source of
her problem. The moment she achieved an altered state
through meditation, Joni began to have clear, sharp, and
colorful visions of herself traveling across Alaska's barren
snow-covered country with her fur-trading husband and
four-year old son, Andrigo. They were of Spanish descent
and were changing homesteads. They were transporting
all their belongings, as well as Andrigo, on a home-made
wooden and leather sled which they had built together.

Suddenly the skies turned gray, and it became dark as
night outside. A gust of wind almost tore the sled they
were pulling behind them out of their hands. She could
see nothing except a gray, swirling haze of driven snow.
They stumbled forward pushing against the wind unable
to hear themselves speak amidst the blare of sounds that
was pouring from the blizzard. Snow drove into their
faces. Screaming in wild rage, the blizzard hurled itself
with the force of a hurricane across the barren land. It
whirled hard packed drifts into frenzied motion. The
blizzard raged unabated. They became exhausted from its
effects and stopped amidst the mountains for shelter only
to discover Andrigo missing from the sled. The ravaging
wind had ripped Andrigo out of his harness.

At this time Joni began sobbing so hard she had trouble
verbalizing. She then continued to relate their frantic
attempt to retrace their tracks only to find the blizzard's

raging wind had buried all signs of life. They continued to search in helpless desperation until they collapsed with fatigue. When they resumed their search they found Andrigo's frozen body buried in a snow drift. Andrigo was dead. Joni sobbed hysterically as she fell to her knees and drew Andrigo's lifeless body to her chest. She sobbed for hours as she knelt on the frozen ground with Andrigo in her arms. She then cried out, "I'm sorry, Andrigo, I did not hear you!" In the reliving Joni could hear Andrigo's pleading voice cry out for help, "Mama", after he was swept off the sled by the raging blizzard. This was a cry for help she was unable to hear in the original experience.

When Joni returned to her present life, and after she composed herself, we processed what she had experienced. We discussed how she had carried her grief in her frozen knees and manifested the energy negatively from one lifetime into another. She also experienced the awareness that Andrigo is her youngest child in this lifetime, a child toward whom she feels very protective.

In the next session Joni related that the evening of the past life recall, she limped from pain in both her legs. She felt unable to support herself on them and had to elevate them. She felt painful tingling sensations from her thighs to her toes throughout the evening. That night she found herself unable to sleep comfortably. This experience was the thawing out of her legs and knees as she had held Andrigo kneeling on the frozen earth. The thawing was a dissolving of the grief, a letting go of the past.

Since this past life recall Joni reports her knees have been 90% pain free. She has had no need for knee supporters on which she frequently depended. The majority of her symptoms remitted immediately after this past life experience. Joni is persistent and continues to work with this karmic pattern to replace the other 10% of the grief she still carries in her knees for Andrigo.

Case II - A Case of Detachment

Ruth was a professional woman in her forties who had not had a loving and supportive relationship with a man even with her husband who died unexpectedly several years ago. She longed for someone to love. She perceived herself as having a limited range of affect. She prematurely aborted her emotional responsivity. She felt "frozen" and "cold". She spoke about feelings in a detached way.

I guided Ruth through a meditation and imaging technique. In this relaxed state, guided imagery helped her access a past life. I asked her to focus on the experience, which caused her to freeze her emotions and lose her range of affect. Since the archetype of reincarnation is circular, I do not focus on the first cause but rather on the transition from a higher state to a lower state. I used Ruth's concern for her induction.

Initially, Ruth could see nothing. As I asked her to go back in time, within seconds images appeared and began to intensify. I followed her in her internal scenario and became intensely involved in sharing her energy field. This allowed me to ask the right questions that would take her to critical issues.

Ruth accessed a past life as a female scholar when intellectual pursuits by women were forbidden. She lived alone in a sparsely decorated hotel room on the third floor with walls lined with book shelves. She lived the life of a hermit in order not to be discovered. One evening three disheveled, ungroomed, long-bearded men broke into her apartment through her bedroom window. The three men initially hugged the wall and danced around each other with mocking gestures. Ruth was still and immobile. The men continued to laugh. The reddish brown haired bearded man approached Ruth and danced around her mockingly. She now stood in shock! He then flung her body on the bed raping his way into her body as the other two now jeered voyeuristically.

Ruth was traumatized into a frozen state. She demonstrated an absence of affect when the ideational content should have necessitated its release. Ruth carried this frozen state with her from one lifetime to another resulting in her limited range of affect in this lifetime. Moments later Ruth experienced the awareness that one of her three rapists was her disheveled adolescent daughter in this lifetime with whom she was having a stormy relationship. The mother and daughter both continuously ran away from each other. The daughter felt unable to look directly at her mother. She was often heard to say, "I just can't look at my mother." When encouraged to do so, she would look at Ruth abruptly, rapidly turn her head, then bow her head in nervous laughter. In inquiring further to the cause of this behavior, the daughter related, "I don't know. It is the way she talks. It's her intelligence." The woman's intellectual pursuits continuously attuned the daughter to the past life when such activities by women were prohibited and she victimized her mother for her scholarly interests. Ruth was astonished how nothing is what it appears to be.

In another past life recall, Ruth was a child locked in a dark room, left alone, abandoned, and disoriented. She eventually lost consciousness and died. At the moment before her spirit passed from her body, she asked, "Why me?" Ruth stated she frequently has asked herself that question in this lifetime.

We processed these recalls and used them as a referent basis for her treatment. She saw clearly the trauma, abandonment, and sense of violation she carried with her through many lifetimes. Taking proper responsibility for these experiences as belonging to the past, Ruth was able to view her daughter in a clearer perspective understanding the guilt from which her daughter operated. Ruth had been unable to change her response style toward her daughter until this reliving. Through this recall, Ruth became more attuned to living in the present and finding meaning in what was in her present world. The relationship between mother and daughter improved temporally associated with the past life recall. No longer did they run away from one another and the daughter dramatically improved her grooming.

Having been the protagonist of her own story, Ruth reported starting to feel "lighter", enjoying quiet time in reading and meditation, and she was demonstrating a wider range of affect. She understood clearly how these psychic residues from previous lifetimes had blocked emotional release. This understanding brought about this releasement. She became centered and serene.

When one is doing a "work-out" such as Ruth's, one is "skimming the fat." What is below is the true person. The subconscious obscured it with this reliving. The essence is what's underneath. In a relaxed, meditative state, the mental consciousness automatically produces a series of images which reflect current life issues. By respecting Ruth's psychic reality, in this remembered state, the trauma could be released. However, this insight is not an end in itself. It's aim is psychic-spiritual development. As Ruth masticated this recovered information mentally, she uncrammed her consciousness of the imbalance resulting from this experience, and began living a life of positive energy.

There are thousands of past lifetimes oscillating with our present life from moment to moment. They oscillate together on a basic frequency. This frequency which penetrates consciousness is a part of everyone's struggle in joining the duality of ourselves, physical and spiritual.

Case III - A Case of Betrayal

Jacob, a therapist in his late thirties, entered therapy because he felt preoccupied with the word "betrayal" within the last three weeks. He said he had a sense that something vital was brewing for him. He found himself significantly attuned to any approximations of betrayals among his patients, his friends, and within himself toward others. He experienced himself as hyperalert to potentially betraying situations.

Jacob was in excellent mental, physical and spiritual health and highly respected in his community both professionally and socially. His life's devotion was the service of others. Jacob was also a very proficient and experienced meditator having meditated daily for over ten years. Consequently, after an explanation of his feelings and attitudes, I guided Jacob into the alpha state to facilitate the recovery of memories and to deepen the understanding of his presenting concern. I used some key words to help deepen his state and reminded Jacob that his Inner Mind knew the answer.

I asked Jacob to repeat the word "betrayal" out loud several times. Then with that thought I asked him to put all the energy that he could into it and let that thought take him back in time and through space. With that facilitation, Jacob immediately began to experience vivid imagery. He saw himself sitting quietly in his living room reading a book. I asked him the title of the book. He said, *The True life of Jesus of Nazareth*. He reported being more than half way through the book. I inquired what page he was reading. He quickly reported page 280. I asked him to read from that page and he proceeded to do so. As he read the verse, "This is the man, said Judas, as he pointed at Jesus. Seize him", Jacob's body went into convulsive sobbing so that his eyelids were so greatly swollen and he could no longer see through his tears. He then cried in agony, "Could I possibly have been the one to have betrayed Jesus! Could I possibly have been Judas!" His question was a statement.

At that point, Jacob experienced a sharp pain in his left side which started from his hip to his chest. He fell to his knees and began hyperventilating in the midst of uncontrollable sobbing. He was too fatigued from the experience to process this recall in this session. However, Jacob related having retired to bed early that evening because of fatigue only to be awakened an hour and a half later with an enormous pain in his rectum. He rushed to the bathroom, feeling faint, placing his head against the floor to prevent a black-out. This weakened state was followed by a tremendous rectal purging of black fluid so that he could not imagine his body containing such a large amount of waste. He felt enormously weak and returned to bed only to experience a second rectal purging two hours later.

Upon awakening in the morning, Jacob felt weak and exhausted, but by noon he was clear and energized so that he taught himself a complete new piece of music on the piano. Jacob had related that he had been blocked with his music for the last three weeks.

After this past life recall, Jacob felt clear and transcended. The negative portion of that cycle had come to an end. The reliving had provided a cathartic release and freedom from his recent obsession. The thoughts which brought him into therapy no longer intruded on his daily life. Furthermore, Jacob reported experiencing a greater loyalty to everyone and everything around him. Jacob experienced a step-up in his consciousness as a result of this reliving. It deepened his spiritual path.

Case IV - A Case of Obsession

Danielle was a professional woman in her forties. She related a lifelong experience of healthy interpersonal relationships with both genders. She had a strong marriage and a healthy family relationship. Consequently, she felt troubled and baffled that she was finding herself in a tremendously dysfunctional interpersonal relationship with a male colleague with whom she had only a brief acquaintance. It was draining her physically and emotionally since the man was telephoning her daily, sometimes two or three times in a day, and sending her expensive gifts. Danielle remarked that this man was a brilliant scholar who had made an international contribution and appeared highly spiritually evolved apart from this obsession. This man's obsession seemed incongruent to Danielle with her perception of him.

Danielle was well grounded in her belief in past lives and was eager to engage in recall activity. She reported that recently whenever she spoke with this man she would develop a pain in her neck that she could not eliminate through various efforts. I asked Danielle to close her eyes and do some deep breathing. She quickly achieved a highly relaxed state being an experienced meditator. I asked Danielle to take her awareness to her neck and repeat, "You're a pain in the neck!" After several repetitions Danielle began to yell, "You are hurting me, let me go, let me go!" I asked her what she was experiencing. She reported that a man named Randolph had his hands around her neck and was choking her.

Danielle was recalling a past life where she was a call girl to wealthy business men. Randolph was a steady customer whenever he was in town.

Danielle came from a large poverty stricken family which struggled to keep food on the table. She was the oldest of seven children and the father was deceased. She felt an aching responsibility for her mother and her siblings. Being of high intelligence Danielle learned early in life that men appreciated looking at her and frequently commented on her beautiful, dark ethnic skin and jet black long flowing hair. At age eighteen she began to use her looks to feed her family. She became a call girl to travelling executives.

Danielle worked her profession for seven years after which time she fell in love with a man who was not a customer. They wanted to marry. When she informed Randolph that she was leaving the business and she would no longer be available to him, he entered into a rage and became physically and verbally violent with Danielle. He began to squeeze his hands tightly around her neck reminding her that he was responsible for most of her family's comforts and her brother's education. He threatened the life of the man she loved. Danielle struggled her way free from the suffocating grip of this raging, possessive, power hungry man who wanted to own her. She fell to the floor and wept.

At this point I asked Danielle to move ahead five years

and see if she had married. She said, "No, because of continuous threats from Randolph." Randolph demanded that she see no one else but him as he became her sole supporter. Danielle went through the motions of her work but her spirit died.

Upon this recall, Danielle's neck pain disappeared. As she processed the recall she realized that as Randolph owned her in a previous lifetime, he was now replaying an old tape attempting to buy her with expensive gifts and being demanding of her time. Danielle could understand that she found herself in a past life with the same person in a different power class and sexual constellation, ie. a mistress. This reliving released all the blocked energy relating to the old trauma. Danielle also developed the awareness that the man with whom she fell in love in the previous lifetime was her husband in her present life.

Danielle discussed her reliving with her male acquaintance knowing that he was also solidly grounded in past life recall. He accepted this recall and revealed having felt jealous of her present husband whom he had never met. "This reliving answers many things", he told Danielle. After some weeks of working through this reliving together, Danielle and her male acquaintance released this past life. They have since been able to move forward in mutual support of one another's professional work. Danielle reports a move from an obsessional path to a spiritual path.

The experiences that occur during past life therapy cover a wide spectrum of depth and intensity. Sometimes these experiences are gentle and subtle. Othertimes, they are overwhelming, painful and intense. Each time, however, they are transcending. They are normal and natural manifestations of the human psyche, as the seeker of truth progresses in the desire to know of Self!

Past Life Therapy is a method
by which we stop being
someone we thought we were
And become our True Selves.

M. Teri Daunter

Chapter Eleven

PAST LIFE THERAPY AND PSYCHOANALYSIS

Past life therapy and psychoanalysis make significant contributions to the psychology of character. They both consider origin and development of styles. Both philosophies understand the human organism as being a complicated energy system and help to rearrange these energy patterns of thought and emotion . Both systems support the organism as being the same source of energy as universal energy. This energy is defined as psychic energy which performs psychological work. They both speak of the transformation of psychic energy into bodily energy by the stimulation of a pattern of energy waves. Past life therapists and psychoanalysts believe in repressed memories, memories unavailable or forgotten by the person. Their central concepts are conscious/unconscious processes although they each describe these concepts differently. Despite the difference in the language, both systems attempt to discover determining forces in personality that are not directly known to the individual. Both systems are dedicated to teaching an individual about what is going on below the level of awareness by re-arranging energy patterns of the mind, body, and emotions in order to create ease rather than disease. In looking at some key concepts through both systems which are involved in the development of personality, we can see the similarities, differences, and relationship between past life therapy and psychoanalysis.

The Oedipus Complex in psychoanalysis is viewed as the nucleus of neurotic conflict. In its simplified form, the Oedipus Complex is the case of a child at a very early age (around 5 years of age) who develops an object-cathexis for the parent of the opposite gender. The boy cathexis toward his mother with a specific focus on the mother's breast. The girl cathexis toward the father with a specific penis envy, according to psychoanalytic thinking. As the child's sexual wishes for the opposite gender person intensifies, the same gender parent is perceived as an obstacle and interference by the child. An affectionate relationship toward the opposite gender parent and an ambivalent relationship with the same gender parent persist in the content of the simple Oedipus Complex. Freud further posits that these dynamics create such significant anxiety that the child defends himself by repressing these incestuous desires, and this is how the Oedipus Complex disappears.

Past life therapy makes us aware that we have known our children in previous lifetimes. Consequently, a woman's son today may have been her husband in a previous lifetime. This explains why this particular child would experience erotic feelings and thoughts toward his mother in this lifetime and feel jealousy toward the father. The son wishes to be exclusive with the mother as a result of the frequency of energy regenerated from a previous lifetime. If the child and/or mother have no grounding in past life work, they will experience many mixed emotions. However, with an understanding of interdimensional concepts they would realize that these forbidden feelings are of a positive nature stemming from a lifetime of having been passionate lovers in a previous incarnation. They can then take responsibility for these experiences as belonging to a previous lifetime and move ahead.

This position in past life theory explains why some children struggle with the Oedipus Complex and others do not. Every parent-child relationship does not evolve from a similar background of having been lovers in past lives. Such variabilities in the Oedipus Complex were difficult for Freud to explain. Past life philosophy makes clearer the Oedipus Complex and implements it toward spiritual evolution.

Psychoanalysis defines cases of gender dysphoria as transsexualism. In most of these cases, psychoanalytic treatment is unsuccessful and at best brings about an adjustment to a lifestyle which does not feel inherently natural. A female may feel "trapped" in a male body or vice versa. For many it is a life threatening situation as they feel helpless to escape this cage of life. Suicide is frequently entertained. Other times, it leads to homosexual tendencies in adult life. For many the solution is electrolysis, analysis, and hormonal therapy with an endocrinologist to prepare one for cross-living. After a year of cross-living, the person is evaluated for sex reassignment surgery which is typically a series of fifteen or more major surgeries over a period of several years in an attempt to change the sexual composition of an individual. In this way, it is believed, an individual can be made whole.

Past life theory asserts another position for pulling oneself out of such darkness and into the light. Past life philosophy states that more likely a series of lives, but not all lives, are lived in one gender. However, when too much maleness or femininity exists in an individual's psyche, a changeover takes place to establish balance in conjunction with the concept of polarity. In some cases this change-over results in gender-identity confusion and an uncertainty as to which gender one belongs. Treatment consists of helping the individual access the lifetimes when this changeover took place to provide clarity and perspective on the present experience that in a previous incarnation the individual was a member of the opposite gender and still clings tenaciously to that role.

Psychoanalysis views anxiety neurosis as the experience of leaving the old and familiar for the new and unfamiliar. When anxiety becomes great, an individual becomes fixated on an old way of life rather than progress forward. Psychoanalysis posits that the prototype of all later anxiety reactions stem from the birth trauma - the separation of the infant from the familiar relationship of the mother.

Past life theory views the cause of anxiety as an individual's initial separation from Infinite Creative Intelligence either in the present life or previous lifetimes. Therefore, the more spiritually evolved one becomes and the closer one moves toward the Source, the less anxious one becomes.

Psychoanalysis views the transference phenomenon as the human tendency to personalize any relationship. This phenomenon involves unconscious content activated into the present moment which results in conflicting and unassimilated feelings about an individual in the past that interfere and distort our perception about a person or situation. Transference can be to a person, place or thing and stirs up conflicts and insights.

Past life therapy recognizes these affinities to persons, places or things and bases these acquaintances potentially on this lifetime as well as previous incarnations. As these relivings break open, they help a person resolve issues of personal identity, functioning in the world, and spiritual potentialities.

Psychoanalysis explains an obsession as an idea, emotion or impulse that continuously forces itself into consciousness even though one does not want it. As long as an obsession does not interfere with normal functioning, then it is not problematic. However, pathological obsessions are often chronic and harass a person's mental functioning. The individual experiences little conscious control and feels manipulated and maneuvered by these unwelcome thoughts. Obsessions typically appear in sensory images and are highly charged with emotions. They can be of an intellectual nature resulting in preoccupations with existential and metaphysical issues such as life's purpose and meaning. Obsessions can be inhibiting, resulting in extreme scruples and fears and somatic complaints which restrict a person's day-to-day functioning. Obsessions can also come in the form of impulsive ideas which lead to harmful action. Psychoanalysis interprets obsessions as a defense against aggressions or sexual impulses and most often related to the Oedipus Complex.

Past life therapy views obsessions as input from a transmitter (mind) that is out-of-phase with the primal causal transmitter, Infinite Creative Intelligence, in the Plasma Field. These negative out-of-phase signals create distress

171

in an individual. They become masks for maintaining balance and organization in an individual's present life. The mask becomes his world as he is attuned through his obsession to his past in one or more life situations. In other words, the particular masked role the individual is playing in the present is being transmitted from a previous lifetime. The nature of therapy is to present the masks to the person in his natural habitat, a previous lifetime in which the mask was initially donned. Then he can take the mask off. This separation, however, cannot be done instantaneously because the obsessions come from different points of time. It may require accessing several lifetimes before all the obsessions are eliminated.

Regarding obsessions, Dr. Charles L. Spiegel, psychologist and past life therapist, states that "man on the third dimensional earth worlds is constantly receiving signals from a fourth dimensional world. However, in these worlds there are many individuals who are themselves already obsessed from previous life experiences lived on earth worlds and are not in tune with their higher consciousness, and the higher Spiritual Forces. Hence, reception by any individual who had some association with the actual entity who does not now occupy a physical anatomy, is out-of-phase or is distorted; the signal contains a cacophony or mixture of lowercase signals, containing obsessive thought forms."

Negative thought waves, then, started by an individual in the universe will be received by a mental receiving station in the fourth dimension of the same frequency and caliber. Minds with similar frequencies are attracted together. An individual, therefore, is subject to numerous low frequency thought currents if his mind is not in tune with Infinite Creative Intelligence, or if he is not hooked up to higher vibrations than those of negations.

It is important to remember that communication is a movement of energy affecting all our thoughts and actions. Energy is electronic wave forms functioning on a particular frequency. By understanding this principle and analyzing the negative content of our thoughts, such as the low frequency energy of obsessions, we can break down the corrosive effect of the negative thought form or signal, spurious energy that is non-progressive. This is how you use your electronic device, your receiver, your mind, so that you can understand the principle of healing. These spurious non-progressive wave forms can be seen on an oscilloscope. Irregular wave forms are unintelligent wave forms (obsessions). The more beautiful the clarity of the picture, the more intelligent is the sine wave. Sine wave movement of energy can be represented in picture and sound on a television monitor for analysis and study.

Psychoanalysis views dreams as wish fulfillment, and that we dream about what we want. In dreams we disguise repressed infantile wishes (often sexual). Later in his life Freud became more attuned to the presence of psychical phenomena in dreams and stated, "If I had my life to live over again, I should devote myself to psychical research rather than psychoanalysis."

Past life theory holds that dreams are glimpses of past lifetimes and forecasters of our future. Dreams are representation of the psyche through which we find solutions to our present day problems.

Past life therapy and psychoanalysis both view meditation as a process for widening one's field of vision and tapping into areas outside our immediate awareness. The unconscious of psychoanalysis, however, is a cauldron of primitive drives and urges. Past life therapy views the unconscious as containing the polarized dimensions of each individual, the best and the worst of all past and present life experiences. Past life therapy makes use of meditation for spiritual growth. It views meditation as expanding consciousness toward the Divine as a guiding influence. Psychoanalysis, on the other hand, views and uses meditation to expand consciousness in the direction of repressed sexual urges in order to gain mastery over these drives. Both disciplines agree that meditation redistributes psychic energy so that the existing difficulties become unimportant by losing their energetic dominance. The cumulative effect of meditation purges negative influences as part of its healing effect. Consequently, proficient and effective daily meditators are practicing treatment and prevention.

The point of departure in these two therapeutic philosophical systems is found in the breadth and vision of the mind. Freudian psychoanalytic philosophical theory stops short of a full explanation of the mind. It emphasizes an overwhelming third-dimensional model of the afflictions of man's psyche, a model based on rigid categories of time, space, and person. It is painfully narrow and limited to postnatal biography. Past life therapy sees mind as transcending the third dimensional self and envelopes many lives with past, present, and future times blended together. Furthermore, the aggregate of psychological energies which make up the individual personality of psychoanalysis as it appears to exist in a practical or moral sense in everyday life does not constitute in rebirth philosophy the "spirit" in any metaphysical interpretation of the word. Despite their differences, the best in both disciplines can work together for the betterment of humanity's spiritual evolution rather than to criticize that which we do not know.

Destiny is not a matter of chance;
it is a matter of choice.
It is not a thing to be waited for;
it is a thing to be achieved.

William Jennings Bryan

Chapter Twelve

THE KARMIC RHYTHMS OF LIFE

Dr. Ian Stevenson, the Freud of this coming century, psychiatrist, and Carlson Professor of Psychiatry at the University of Virginia Medical School, has published five volumes through the University of Virginia Press of case histories on children who have described memories of former lives. His cases in his files now total over 2,000. Several of his articles have been published in the Journal of Nervous and Mental Diseases (JNMO). The 165th volume of this highly reputable medical journal, dated September 1977, was almost totally devoted to Dr. Ian Stevenson's research on the rebirth philosophy. Dr. Stevenson is regarded by his colleagues as a psychiatrist of "high integrity" and of "great intellectual ability and high professional standards who takes a most painstaking approach to collection and analysis of raw data."

Dr. Stevenson is mostly interested in reincarnational cases with children between ages two to four because children give a "richness of obscure detail" at a time when they have "limited access to information upon which they could consciously or unconsciously build a case." Furthermore, Dr. Stevenson comments, "many of these cases lend themselves to accurate verification because most of the previous lives terminated only a few years prior to the present incarnation. Consequently, former parents and relatives are still alive to attest to, or contradict what the children say." Dr. Ian Stevenson concludes, "The evidence is so preponderantly in favor of reincarnation that you cannot doubt it if you have anything like an open mind."

Research in past life recall is not new. It was initiated 65 years ago in the United States by a pioneer in past life regression, A. R. Martin. Dr. Stevenson is continuing this research on rebirth philosophy along with many other highly reputable psychologists, psychiatrists, and other professionals in the field. However, Dr. Ernest L. Norman and Ruth E. Norman introduced the scientific study of past life therapy incorporating an interdimensional understanding of science. They have accumulated many thousands of case studies of individuals who successfully healed themselves.

Dr. Ernest L. and Ruth E. Norman established the Unarius Academy of Science in 1954, advancing an understanding of the nature of consciousness through their important work in the psychology and physics of reincarnation. The research along with the wealth of clinical cases available to us internationally takes us beyond a neutral position on past life recall and invites investigation. Furthermore, 40 million Americans, one-quarter of the adult population, are grounded in rebirth philosophy according to recent polls. Despite these figures, we know that truth does not stand or fall by a show of hands.

An open-minded inquirer will examine ideas which may deepen his vision and lead further toward spiritual illumination. With the multitude of growing evidence available that reincarnations occur, we need to explore what value has rebirth and what role do the karmic rhythms of life play in reincarnation.

The purpose of existence is growth and creative expression. The unpardonable sin of our multidimensional universe is stagnation. Immortality, therefore, gives us the assurance of progressive improvement. From incarnation to incarnation we transmigrate the moral and intellectual essences which have shaped our spirit. Life is a proportional facsimile of one's efforts in a previous lifetime. The character that shapes a newborn is thus the karma of an endless series of past experiences. Recall enhances this experience by giving it meaning. Without past life recall it is similar to starting to read a novel in chapter twelve unaware of the development of the characters or plot since you missed the previous chapters.

This life, therefore, is a fragment of a long, long story. Death is an end to a chapter, but not the end of the story. Recovering the rest of the story through past life recall unfolds a richer pattern of experience by analyzing the karmic rhythms of life.

Karma is the moral law of the universe. It is a Sanskrit word which means "action" and is a central concept to be found in The Bhagavad-Gita and the Upanishads, Hindu spiritual works which have transcended cultural folkways and mores, have expanded beyond cultural boundaries, and are regarded with imperishable significance in the Western countries. Karma is the rhythmic dynamic force of the universe interweaving all the forces of nature. Its premise is that every effect has its cause, and every cause has its determinate effect. This concept extends to our physical, mental, and spiritual lives and commits us to complete personal responsibility. All the aggregate effects of karma, the energy of our destiny, form the substance upon which our next life is based. Disease is caused by the negative results of past deeds in previous lives. It is the outworking of energy patterns. Any attempt to escape the inexorable law of karma entangles you further. The only prevailing law over karma is love!

Karmic law restores balance and harmony in the vibrational disturbance of both the physical and moral world by rearranging the energy patterns of mind and body. This natural cycle of cause and effect extends beyond time and space into our many lifetimes. Anything of either positive or negative frequency initiated in the third dimensional world is eternally linked to our spirit and is destined for readjustment in another lifetime. The akashic record is the data bank for karma. This universal cyclic law brings everything into equilibrium so that 'what you sow, so shall you reap.'

The law of karma restores spiritual self-reliance. In karmic law no one can forgive you as in many religious escapist doctrines. Neither will you suffer eternal damnation for your acts. However, you will be unable to escape the consequences of your own actions since karmic vibrations are deeply embedded within your being. The law of exact compensation in the universe will not allow you to run away from yourself. The universal law of cause and effect emphasizes personal responsibility not external authority.

This karmic pattern then is a governing factor in the

rebirth process since we enter life reaping the opportunities or limitations which we sowed in a previous lifetime. This inherited pattern is what must be conquered in order to develop our Infinite Creative Intelligence.

Karma, however, is not a blind implacable determinism rendering one into a helpless pawn. This misconception of 'fate' and fear of losing external control over their congregations is what led early Christians and Judaic church leaders to exclude these established and well accepted teachings from church doctrine in 593 A.D. at the Second Council of Constantinople. These concepts were a fact of life to them until the sixth century A.D. As a matter of survival the official Christian church avoided the reincarnation doctrine and would not allow belief in reincarnation to take hold in its followers.

Early religious leaders further feared that individuals would postpone and procrastinate their spiritual works under the premise of another chance in another lifetime. This could be true if one disregarded or excluded karmic law. Any narrowing of consciousness and limitations of a third-dimensional existence must be discharged through an experience of equivalent action. Every action, thought or emotion of pain or suffering directed toward another human being, animal, or thing will become a cause, the effect of which will be experienced in an equal and opposite reaction on oneself in a future lifetime. Who would want to entertain a new life with such conditioning and predisposition?

Karma is like a card game. Although one is dealt a particular hand, one has numerous choices in how to play that hand! Consequently, the source of karma is constantly guided by one's choices. If we fail the challenge of our choices we lower our frequency vibrational rate. If we embrace the test of our choice we raise our frequency level. We are always forming and reforming ourselves by every thought, action and emotion. What one does, however, is not as important as the attitude by which one does it.

We must not jump to conclusions that poor life circumstances are debts for bad karma in a previous lifetime. A spirit may have intentionally chosen painful circumstances in a lifetime in order to accelerate his spiritual development. It is critical, then, that we do not judge another's karma.

We keep ourselves bound to karma when we hold a fragmentary view of the world and perceive ourselves as separated from our environment. This is an illusion. It is an intellectual concept which has no reality. The oneness of all things and events is a constant sensation and is driven by karma, the never-ending chain of cause and effect.

The awareness of rebirth philosophy changes our quality of life. It makes one more adaptable as one realizes that this lifetime opportunity is one of many more to come. We understand that life's circumstances are temporary and transitory.

The motivating force of the spirit is to meet in every experience that which will draw the spirit closer to Itself. Karma then is the development of self. Karma is never between individuals but within ourselves. Other people merely provide the conditions for us to learn our lesson, make our path straight and in keeping with the Source, and to gain self-mastery. In relationships we merely meet ourselves through the law of nature which has no timetable.

In nature nothing is lost. The energy complex is carried to a future life until we penetrate the darkness of our consciousness and rise to the highest level of our Pure Self through the spiritual science of reincarnation, a working principle of spirit evolution in the universe.

PART FIVE

If the doors of perception were cleansed, everything would appear as it is, infinite.

William Blake

Chapter Thirteen

THE PARANORMAL NATURE OF CONSCIOUSNESS

The paranormal, a higher-dimensional intelligence, is a potential ability for the entire human race. We have a responsibillity to use this ability constructively and in the service of mankind. The paranormal state is the innate nature of the consciousness of the human mind. The paranormal is our common spiritual nature. It is our essential identity which is the source of true learning and growth. Direct experience of our true nature fosters self-healing and allows us to facilitate healing in the world.

Our acquired habits are nurtured not natural. Underneath our dispositions nurtured by different cultural conditions are the same natural powers and potentialities. Nurtured differences, therefore, do not equal nature. The former is superficial while the latter is our sameness. The development of our higher attributes, our feeling self, is an evolutionary process, developed over many lifetimes both in the astral and the physical worlds. The paranormal nature of consciousness is the doorway to a higher dimension, providing important information to function more adequately in one's daily life. The mind, which is our consciousness, is the same in all human beings. Consequently, paranormal abilities, the perceiving beyond our five senses, are innate capabilities in each of us and not reserved for the inexplicably favored.

Consciousness is the projection of Infinite Creative Intelligence, a polarized abstraction of the Infinite. Consciousness power originates from where all things originate, from the Infinite. The powers of Infinite Creative Intelligence is reflected as stepped down energy into different vibratory levels, from the paranormal to the normal, so-called physical consciousness. These different vibratory levels make up the universe and correspond to the different segments of our creation. Therefore, what is considered paranormal by different cultural conditions is merely man awakening to his Infinite nature. Paranormal is the non-sensory, non-physical way of communicating between individuals. It is a high vibratory level of functioning and a higher order source of knowledge. This is not happenstance. It is a derivative of a timeless and abstract Infinite. It is a deep connectiveness with a higher order expressed as extra-sensory perception, telepathy, and clairvoyance as in past life recall. Rebirth is as normal a part of human life as biological birth. It is an intrinsic part of the universal scheme of things. However, culture has pathologized the experience. Disregard of the paranormal is a prejudice bred by the error of blaming nature for the products of nurture. To consider only nurtural differences is to negate the interdimensional field force of the mind and the regenerative evolutionary spirit which is the nature of man.

Conventional truth which makes up nurtural differences imprisons us within the norm. However, dealing with things you know without knowing why, takes you beyond nurturing and into the paranormal. Such directly contacted truths are fundamentally transforming and is the knowledge of a greater awareness and knowing. It is an uncovering of something natural that has been covered over by nurtural differences and conditioning. Nurturing is an illusion, and sometimes we have to risk all to find the truth. Reality is in us, not in a text or social conditioning.

Life through nurtural conditioning is a vast and unrelated delusion which forms the destructive potentials of life since it is not a factual continuity of Infinite expressions. It is this hypnotic-trance like condition that has cut us off from the paranormal nature of our consciousness. Nurturance keeps us at an elemental stage of evolution by its sheep-like attitude. We must emancipate ourselves from rote systems and the rhetorical minds which support them if we are ever going to experience the spiritual dance of life. The paranormal is how our two worlds meet. If the paranormal or psychic disposition of a person is to be attained, it can only be done by the elimination of rhetorical elements and robot-like existence which keep one's vibratory level at a lower frequency. A person can develop his mental capacity to extensive proportions and raise his vibratory frequency by living as a creative element functioning reconstructively with the Infinite.

Cultural conditioning short circuits our mind. We need

to set up our mind to listen and bring it into practice through calmness and awareness in order to contact the layers of mind inside us. Mind, our consciousness, is an interdimensional processing system. It is a permanent storage of everything we have ever experienced. Mind gathers all information while brain merely interprets it. Consciousness, therefore, is not the product of brain function. It is consciousness which relates to everything one knows since the person became an entity.

We develop paranormal ability by knowing about the Infinite and becoming selective on the basis of frequency attunement. By mindfully accepting or rejecting frequencies constantly oscillating into our psychic anatomy, we attain a higher functioning way of life. The spiritual dance of life achieved through the understanding of the science of life is the climax to one's search. Interdimensional understanding allows one to direct the vehicle of life in a progressive evolution. The paranormal then becomes the practical reality of life, a life lived harmoniously with the Infinite, a regenerative principle of life, receiving and recreating what it has received. The paranormal, then, is the progressive evolution of, and living as, an equalized oscillating function with the Infinite Creative Intelligence which then becomes a part of our every thought and action. It requires one to desist from age-old habits and conditioning and develop a new life technocracy. The principle in action in the paranormal is the Infinite. Dedicate yourself, then, to the new proposition of life, an understanding of the Infinite, and the logic and reason of life!

Cultural powers hinder man's inner self by creating separations and boundries which are illusory. Originality achieved through the paranormal is repressed since it may hamper the efficiency of standardized society. The paranormal, however, is not to be accepted indiscriminately with the naive inexperience of the infant, nor is it to be discarded as nonsense. An evolved individual with the depth of a spiritually mature adult becomes attuned to his findings. Not only do we need to be critical of what comes in from the outside world, but we need to be accepting of what comes up from our inner world that contains the reality of spirit.

These pages have been written to present new information on the capacity of consciousness and conscious change and its application to the lived life. It is an attempt to import some knowledge about our minds that is mostly lacking in our third-dimensional world. A radical and rapid revision is essential about Consciousness, in order to better understand the delicacy and absolute necessity to appropriately direct our minds in order to allow for the larger movement of spirit in our lives.

Every ending

is a

Beginning

Thomas Moore

EPILOGUE

T.S. Eliot observed, "Humankind cannot bear very much reality." The very sensitive and potentially controversial nature of the material of this book may stretch the limits of what our cultures perceive as corporeal reality. The common denominator of this book is that there are nonordinary states of consciousness that are healing and transformative and that we are not skin-encapsulated egos. I only wish to make people aware of a wider, more expansive reality so that their lives are not squandered and dissipated.

The world is as one conceives it, and one's conceptions drive, guide, and catapult a person's actions. It is the stretching of one's conceptions that will light one's pathway into Infinity. Therefore, may this book serve as a meditation for souls in process and touch as many lives as possible with a message of the hope and inspiration which ignited my writing. May this book help you to find quiet strength in a very chaotic, turbulent world. May it help you see the light behind the shadows and set your soul on fire.

"The breeze at dawn has secrets to tell you.
Don't go back to sleep.
You must ask for what you really want.
Don't go back to sleep.
People are going back and forth across the doorsill
Where the two worlds touch.
The door is round and open.
Don't go back to sleep."

Rumi

APPENDICES

THE CYCLE OF LIFE

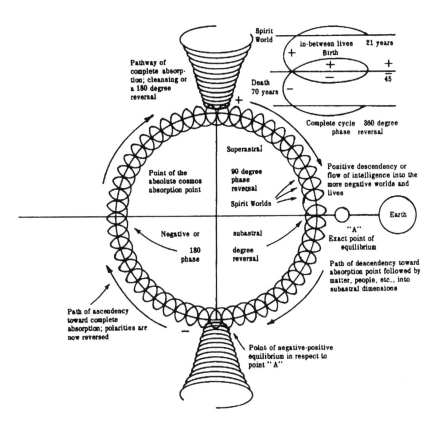

(The cause, purpose and reason for all things: the "Open Sesame" to Creation)
People also ascend via "Spirit Worlds"

Originated by Dr. Ernest L. Norman

EDITING OF THOUGHTS

Purpose:
To probe into the "Stream of Consciousness."
To analyze different bits of life experience.
To integrate these bits into a coherent whole.
To develop clairvoyance and read the past.

Method:
This is an initial exercise in the development of self awareness. It will be a corrective technique and a safeguard that will prevent future re-enactments of those negative life experiences that were the dominant influences of one's past.

It is suggested that you choose one hour from a previous day and proceed to write out a synopsis of the events that took place in that one-hour segment. Be aware of the impressions of your thoughts as you interact with your environment. These are the subtle thought structures that we are learning to recognize. Ask yourself: "Why did I react to the event, the person, place or thing?"

All thoughts are blueprints which contain the building blocks that have caused the disharmony of self and are clues to past life traumas.

This is an initial exercise in the development of awareness and self-analysis. It will be a corrective technique and a safeguard that will prevent the re-enactment of the more negative quotients of experiences that have formed the dominant influences of past expressions in former lives.

Your environment is an out-picturing of the past life experiences which now reside in your psychic anatomy as vortical energy wave forms. It is the screen upon which your past has been pictured and now is out-pictured in the present, inphase with past life experiences.

By becoming aware of the information comprising one's conscious and subconscious thoughts, one's reactions to persons, places, and things, a personal diary can be developed.

In time, through this means, a personal diary can be written that will provide for a greater degree of objectivity in the interrelationship with self.

The physics of reincarnation is, to all intents and purposes, an understanding of the continuity of consciousness. At the same time the continuity of consciousness is contained in thoughts and actions which permeate the sum and substance of each individual's life.

Carrying out the process of this exercise in mind function and learning of the technique of editing your thoughts will put you 'in front of the cart', so to speak, whereby you will be the director of your consciousness and thereby the director of yourself.

Self-Mastery means the recognition of the subconscious reflexes inherent in all life conditions, and their removal. Thereby clear access is made to the Spiritual Dimensions.

10 Steps *To* Help You Begin *To* Improve Your Life

1. Aim High

Set your mind to living with a purpose. Do not let yourself be stopped by the boundary lines that have blocked your inspiration for growth - spiritually and mentally. Self mastery should be one's true aspiration and objective in life!

2. Keep Active Mentally & Physically

The mind is the main generator providing the substance - the nutrient energy - for a healthy physical body. This psychosomatic relationship is an interactive process which is the main controlling force for good mental health. The integration of the Spirit-Mind-Body is the result.

3. Keep A Positive Attitude

Fill your life with concern for others and your creativity.

4. Be Patient

Rome was not built in a day. There are spiritual forces working with you in your desire to better yourself. You are strengthening your mental muscles - the logic and reason of your intelligence, so that you can learn to overcome certain fixed attitudes that have kept you captive in your past!

5. Be Persistent

It will take effort on your part to attain what you aspire to. Your continued efforts will determine the success of your objectives, in whatever manner that you have chosen.

6. Trim The Fat From Negative Mental Attitudes

Such self-centeredness is negative energy that weighs you down, mentally, emotionally, and physically!

7. Let Spirit Work With You

The energy that is the Force of the Cosmos is of an *Infinite Creative Intelligence* which can regenerate the substance of your mind. You can be freed from the shocks and bonds that imprisoned you due to negative past lifetime experiences.

8. Obtain The Necessary Nutrients That Will Recreate And Reinforce A Healthy Mind And Body

These spiritual nutrients are the real components of the "Force" for positiveness - composed of the electromagnetic energies of the all-pervading Infinite Creative Intelligence!

9. Lighten Up

Keep your sense of humor and do not let temporary problems get you down. Laughter has healing properties.

10. Extend The Frontiers Of Your Mind

Begin the study of the Consciousness. Consciousness is the totality of one's awareness and participation in the evolutionary process of living life-after-life, a continuity of consciousness - never ending!

The Psychology of Consciousness is the study of Interactive Interdimensional Energy Forces that are the building blocks for developing a healthy and integrated relationship of the Body, Mind and Spirit.

In essence, when you begin the study of "Self" you are putting-into-action *corrective and preventive* processes which will advance your spiritual development .. upon the pathway of a progressive evolution!

Raise Your Awareness Through Self Analysis

LEARN TO SPOT THE CLUES TO PAST LIFE MEMORIES

1. **Your Special Rapport and Your Reactions to People, Places and Things**
   - Historical Figures
   - Religious Leaders
   - Artists and Art Decor
   - Clothing-food-homes-vacation spots-hobbies, etc.
   - Epic Movies and Plays
   - Fears and Anxieties

2. **Personal Crises Of An Emotional Nature**
   - Physical Problems
   - Dreams
   - Psychological Problems
   - Negative Family Relations
   - Work-related Problems

3. Your Belief Structures

- Be open to *new* concepts that are in advance of dogmatic practices and beliefs
- Learn to question your attitudes and opinions
- Fixed attitudes, opinions and beliefs generate an obsessive and narrow focus of life and cripple one's capability to function with logic and reason.

PAST LIFE THERAPY
A New Science of Life

An Introduction into The Study of Consciousness

There is an urgent need for a drastic revision of existing paradigms (standard models) for psychology, psychiatry, medicine and science.

Our current understanding of the universe - of the nature of reality and most of all of human beings, is superficial, incorrect and incomplete.

Our current perception of reality does not allow for metaphysical-interdimensional experiences. A narrow perception of reality creates illusionary boundary lines because they lack distinction between the past, present and future. The parts of the whole - the interconnectedness of all persons, places and things, is the holographic reality of the electromagnetic nature of energy that is the universal plasma of life. This knowledge, is the missing link that will connect one's self to the higher order of one's consciousness and is the basis for an Interdimensional Physics of Life.

There is now a transformation taking place on Earth,

that is the beginning of a change - the raising of the consciousness of Homo sapiens towards a new paradigm - that of the realization of an interdimensional concept of life which, when realized and put into practice, will eventually change how we look at the world. We will then understand how we are a continuity of the Past, Present and Future, providing a wider perception of the reality of a Space-time Continuum. As a result we will view life from a spiritual bias because our sight will reveal to us the reality of life as it is and has always been of an Infinite Creative Intelligence.

It is the prerogative of all human beings to become aware of the regenerative evolutionary nature of one's self, a creative spark of Infinity. It is our purpose to ever expand our consciousness to become part of the Grand Design of Life and not remain in a fragmented state, separated from the Life Force - the pulsing electromagnetic energy that surrounds each person and interpenetrates the cellular structures of our mental and physical bodies.

It is not natural to be sick. Sickness of the mind and the body is a sign of disease - the separation of the Spiritual components of the mind which results in a blockage of nutrients from entering the Consciousness of the individual. The reasons for sickness - disease in body, mind and spirit are apparent. It is true because individuals have not realized that they have blocked their arteries from receiving the Well Spring of Energy that is continually regenerating the component parts of their psychic-electro-magnetic and physical anatomies, which would result in the healing of one-self.

My Daily Meditation And Centering Night Light

Lord (*Infinite Creative Intelligence*) make me
    an instrument of your peace
Where there is hatred, let me sow love.
    Where there is injury, pardon.
Where there is doubt, faith.
    Where there is despair, hope.
Where there is darkness, light.
    And where there is sadness, hope.

O - Divine Master,
    grant that I may not so much
Seek to be consoled, as to console;
    to be understood, as to understand;
To be loved - as to love;
    For it is in giving, that we receive,
It is in pardoning, that we are pardoned.
And it is in the dying, that we are born
    to eternal life.

        St. Francis of Assisi
       Early proponent of non-local mind

BIBLIOGRAPHY
AND FURTHER READING

Avila, St. Teresa of, *The Interior Castle*, Paulist Press, New York, 1979.

Bods, Murray, *Francis, The Journey and The Dream*, Anthony Messenger Press, 1988.

Borys, Henry James, *The Sacred Fire*, Harper, San Francisco, 1994.

Borysenko, Joan, Ph.D., *Fire In The Soul*, Warner Books, NY, 1993.

Brown, Tom, Jr., *The Vision*, Berkley Books, New York, 1988.

Capra, Fritjof, *The Turning Point*, Bantam Book, New York, 1982.

Cayce, Hugh Lynn, *The Edgar Cayce Reader*, Constellation International Edition, New York, 1969.

Chopra, Deepak, *Quantum Healing*, Bantam Books, New York, 1989.

Cranston, Sylvia and Carey Williams, *Reincarnation*, Julian Press, New York, 1984.

Davidson, John, *Subtle Energy*, D.W. Daniel Co., Ltd., England, 1987.

Davies, Paul, *God and the New Physics*, Simon & Schuster, New York, 1983.

Doores, Gary, *What Survives*, Jeremy P. Tarcher, Inc., Los Angeles 1990.

Dossey, Larrey, M.D., *Meaning and Medicine*, Bantam Books, NY, 1992.

Dossey, Larry, *Recovering The Soul*, Bantam Books, New York, 1989.

Ferguson, Robert A., *New Way to Mystic Power and Prosperity*, Parker Publishing Co. New York, 1979.

Freud, Sigmund, *On Dreams*, W.W. Norton & Co, New York, 1952.

Fritjof, Capra, *The Tao of Physics*, Bantam Books, New York, 1976.

Grof, Stanislaw, Ph. D. and Christina, *The Stormy Search For Self*, Tarcher/Perigee, Los Angeles, CA, 1992.

Hall, Calvin S. and Vernon J. Nordley, *A Primer of Jungian Psychology*, New American Library, New York, 1973.

Herman, Willis and Howard Rheingold, *Higher Creativity*, Noetic Science Book, California, 1984.

Hilarion, *The Nature of Reality*, Marcus Books, Toronto, 1979.

Karpinski, Gloria D., *Where Two Worlds Touch*, Ballantine Books, New York, 1990.

Laslow, Leonard, *Healing With Love*, Harper, New York, 1992.

Lederman, Leon, *The God Particle*, Dell Publishing, New York, 1993.

Leichtman, Robert and Carl Jakilese, *Active Meditation*, Ariel Press, Ohio, 1982.

Lucas, Winifred, *Regression Therapy*, Volume 1 & 2, Deep Forest Press, California, 1993.

Millman, Dan, *The Warrior Athlete*, Stillpoint Publishing, New Hampshire, 1979.

Martin, Joel & Patricia Romanowski, *We Don't Die*, Berkley Books, New York, 1988.

Moore, Thomas, *Care of the Soul*, Harper Perennial, New York, 1992.

Newton, Michael, *Journey of Souls*, Llewellyn Publications, Minnesota, 1994.

Nichols, Peter, *Journey to Infinity*, Finbarr International, England, 1992.

Norman, Ruth, *Interdimensional Physics*, Unarius Publications, California, 1989.

Norman, Ernest L., *Infinite Perspectus*, Unarius Publications, California, 1962.

Norman, Ernest L., *Infinite Contact*, Unarius Publications, California, 1960.

Norman, Ruth, *Life, Death, and Immortality*, Unarius Publications, California, 1990.

Norman, Ernest L., *Cosmic Continuum*, Unarius Publications, California, 1960.

Norman, Ruth and Charles Spaegel, *Beginner's Guide to Progressive Evolution*, Unarius Publications, El Cajon, California, 1986.

Norman, Ernest L., *Man, The Evolutionary Regenerative Spirit*, Unarius Publications, California, 1988.

Norman, Ruth E. and Charles Spaegel, *The Last Inca, Atahualpa*, Unarius Publications, California, 1992.

Norman, Ruth and Charles Spaegel, *Principles and Practice of Past life Therapy*, Unarius Publications, El Cajon, California, 1984.

Pagels, Heinz R., *The Cosmic Code*, Bantam Books, New York, 1982.

Perkins, James S, *Through Death to Rebirth*, The Theosophical Publishing House, Illinois, 1961.

Perkins, John, *The World Is As You Dream It*, Destiny Books, Rochester, Vermont, 1994.

Pierre Teilhard de Chardin, *Hymn of the Universe*, Harper Torchbooks, NY, 1961.

Pine-Coffin, R. S., *Saint Augustine Confessions*, Penguin Books, Baltimore, Maryland, 1961.

Rawlings, Maurice, *Beyond Death's Door*, Bantam Book, New York, 1978.

Redfield, James, *The Celestine Prophecy*, Warner Books, NY, 1993.

Roads, Michael, *Journey Into Oneness*, Kramer, Tiburon, CA, 1994.

Roger, John, & Peter Mc Williams, *You Can't Afford The Luxury of a Negative Thought*, Prelude Press, California, 1988.

Spaegel, Charles, *The Psychology of Consciousness*, Unarius Publications, El Cajon, California, 1985.

Siegel, Bernie, M.D., *Love, Medicine and Miracles*, Harper & Row, New York, 1986.

Spiegel, Louis, *The Confessions of I, Bonaparte*, Unarius Publications, El Cajon, California, 1985.

Talbot, Michael, *The Holographic Universe*, Harper, New York, 1991.

Thurman, Robert, *The Tibetan Book of the Dead*, Bantam Books, New York, 1994.

Tipler, Frank, *Physics of Immortality*, Doubleday, New York, 1994.

Trungpa, Chogyam, *Cutting Through Spiritual Materialism*, Shambala Publications, Massachussetts 1973.

Trungpa, Chogyam, *Training The Mind*, Shambala, Boston, 1993.

Windsor, Joan R., *Dreams and Healing*, Berkley Books, New York, 1987.

Zukav, Gary, *The Dancing Wu Li Masters*, Wm. Morrow & Co, New York, 1979.

Zukav, Gary, *The Seat of the Soul*, Fireside, New York, 1989.

INDEX

ORDERING INFORMATION

Please send me the following item(s) by Dr. M. Teri Daunter:

_____ *The Spiritual Dance of Life*
      Hardcover @ $20.00   _____

_____ *The Spiritual Dance of Life*
      Softcover @ $16.00   _____

_____ Training Course in Meditative
      Imagery @ $10.00   _____
      (audio instructional tape)

              Subtotal   _____

              6% tax   _____

Add Shipping & Handling:
Book $3.90, Tape $2.50, Both $6.40   _____
(Add $1.00 for each additional book or tape)

              TOTAL   _____

All prices in U.S. currency

Please check method of payment
All orders must be prepaid and include postage & handling

☐   Check enclosed (Payable to **MOBIUS PUBLISHING**)

Charge my   ☐ Visa   ☐ Mastercard

Account # _/_/_/_/   _/_/_/_/   _/_/_/_/   _/_/_/_/

Exp. Date _/_/ _/_/

Signature _____

Date _____

Mail to: **MOBIUS PUBLISHING**
         Post Office Box 2457
         Petoskey, MI 49770

Fax orders to: 1-616-348-0904

Please ship to:

Name _____

Address _____

City _____State _____ Zip _____

Daytime Pho # _____Evening Pho # _____

ORDERING INFORMATION

Please send me the following item(s) by Dr. M. Teri Daunter:

_____ *The Spiritual Dance of Life*
       Hardcover @ $20.00   _____

_____ *The Spiritual Dance of Life*
       Softcover @ $16.00   _____

_____ Training Course in Meditative
       Imagery @ $10.00   _____
       (audio instructional tape)

               Subtotal   _____

               6% tax   _____

Add Shipping & Handling:
Book $3.90, Tape $2.50, Both $6.40   _____
(Add $1.00 for each additional book or tape)

              TOTAL   _____

            All prices in U.S. currency

Please check method of payment
All orders must be prepaid and include postage & handling

☐ Check enclosed (Payable to **MOBIUS PUBLISHING**)

Charge my   ☐ Visa   ☐ Mastercard

Account # _/_/_/_/ _/_/_/_/ _/_/_/_/ _/_/_/_/

Exp. Date _/_/ _/_/

Signature _____

Date _____

Mail to: MOBIUS PUBLISHING
        Post Office Box 2457
        Petoskey, MI 49770

Fax orders to: 1-616-348-0904

Please ship to:
Name _____
Address _____
City _____ State ____ Zip _____
Daytime Pho # _____ Evening Pho # _____